About the author ...

Jane Sen is one of Britain's most original chefs. She has had twenty years of experience cooking professionally in a wide variety of situations. She has travelled extensively, working with chefs all over the world, and this has enabled her to gain a detailed knowledge of many of the world's greatest cuisines. These include Indian, Thai, French, Italian, Chinese and Japanese – and the list goes on. In recent years her food has become greatly in demand by everybody from royalty to rock stars. Jane is now using her inimitable style and unique skills to address the subject of wholefood cookery and the nutritional impact of different diets.

The Healing Foods Cookbook

The Vegan Way to Wellness

Jane Sen

Thorsons

Thorsons
An imprint of HarperCollins*Publishers*
77–85 Fulham Palace Road,
Hammersmith, London W6 8JB

The Thorsons website address is: www.thorsons.com

First published by Thorsons 1996.
This edition 2000.

10 9 8 7 6 5 4 3 2 1

© Jane Sen 1996, 2000

Jane Sen asserts the moral right to be identified as
the author of this work

A catalogue record of this book is available
from the British Library

ISBN 0 00 710816 8

Printed and bound in Great Britain by Scotprint

My love, as ever, to the inspirational Penny Brohn

Contents

Introduction

The extraordinary influence that the food we eat can exert over our health is now an accepted part of our lives. This, despite often confusing and conflicting information from experts, science and the media. However there are some areas in which they are all in unanimous agreement, and when you need to feel confident about making changes to your way of eating, the areas of agreement are the best place to start.

Our food can greatly improve our chances of living a full and healthy life. We can prevent the onset, or manage the symptoms, of many of the major health problems that cause so much suffering. There is good research into how diet can affect our chances of developing cancer, heart disease, diabetes, Alzheimer's disease, asthma, and allergic reactions, and how we may successfully control painful menstruation or a difficult menopause, or use our diet to delay or avoid many of the signs of ageing.

The research is complex and diverse, and in my work and teaching sessions, a point that very quickly becomes obvious is that we cannot stay in good health by merely understanding the science. However convinced we may be that there is something in this *'you are what you eat'* approach, it is absolutely no use whatsoever unless we do actually <u>eat</u> the foods that the evidence is proving will make a difference.

Over many years of cooking – professionally, for loved ones, and especially in my work at the

Bristol Cancer Help Centre – I have found one supremely important element in relation to food: everything about it should be a pleasure. Cooking, preparing, serving and, of course, eating should evoke a sense of delight, excitement and interest. Hippocrates' famous statement about 'food being medicine' is inspiring only when everything to do with it doesn't feel or taste like medicine.

The recipes in this book have been chosen in order to give some inspiration and new ideas which, along with some simple techniques, will ensure that even your first few attempts will produce something delicious enough for you to want to try again. I hope that with encouragement you will begin to find your own favourite combinations – confidently chucking in another handful of chopped fresh basil; replacing dried dates with fresh peaches; and simply leaving out the bits you don't fancy. Adventurous experimentation is the key to success here.

When you are using really fresh and whole ingredients, it is honestly very difficult not to enjoy the results – especially when you have cooked and prepared them with a light heart, enjoying the knowledge that very soon your body will start to say 'thank you'. This diet works. You will begin to feel lots better and more energetic. As you begin to care for yourself, you will find you have more enthusiasm for the kitchen. Soaking and cooking those beans will cease to be a boring chore and begin to feel like a positive and creative step towards better health.

One of the main obstacles in the way of making the changes required by this nutritional approach is the challenge of cooking for people other than yourself. Most of us who are trying to find ways of regaining or maintaining our own good health also have to feed other people. I fully realise that being responsible for the children's supper, the family Sunday lunch, entertaining guests – to say nothing of sorting out the packed lunches – means this can seem all too daunting to contemplate. To help with this I have included plenty of 'look-a-like' or familiar sounding recipes to help you negotiate some of the minefields. Believe me, it is possible to produce a delicious 'quiche' using wholewheat pastry and no eggs. There is even life and enjoyment in the dessert department and the cookie jar without recourse to refined sugar.

It takes everyone a little time to adjust the tastebuds to new textures and flavours, but you will feel all the better for doing it. The resultant sense of well-being is immeasurable and the new energy that comes with it gives you an appetite for food and cooking, and gives life itself a new, revived vigour.

The principles

When you study the mass of current research, you find some simple principles, some basic truths, that reoccur continually as essential if we are to stay healthy or regenerate our health.

They are:

- **We should minimise animal produce,** aiming to gain our proteins from plant foods.
- **We need to avoid saturated fats,** aiming to use cold pressed plant oils and increase intake of essential fatty acids.
- **Our food should be whole and unprocessed where possible,** most of what happens to your food after it is harvested, will happen in your kitchen. (This will also mean with less salt and sugar than we have become accustomed to.)
- **Whenever possible, minimise our exposure to toxins,** by using chemical free, organically grown food.
- **Raw foods should be included daily,** fresh fruits and/or salads at each meal.

Put like that it all sounds very simple, and in essence it is simple, but following these guidelines requires skill if the diet is not to become boring and monotonous. It also calls for imaginative preparation, using techniques that may be new to a lot of people. Also, some familiar foods are ruled out altogether. But there are gains as well as losses: you will find that this is an opportunity to try novel tastes and flavours while experimenting with a wider range of different fruits and vegetables, as well as discovering new sauces and spreads along the way.

Vegan

Most people have an idea about what it means to be a vegetarian but few understand what being a vegan implies. This is hardly surprising since even the so-called *Shorter Oxford Dictionary* offers no definition. A vegan diet excludes all animal products. Not only meat, poultry and fish but also cheese, eggs, butter, cream – in other words, all dairy products. This is a big step away from a vegetarian diet because, although vegetarians don't eat the actual animals themselves, they do often eat products that come from animals, like cheese and eggs. This is why restaurants often offer quiche or omelettes as a vegetarian option on their menus. These would be unacceptable to vegans who don't eat animal products. Vegans get their protein requirements from nuts, seeds, beans and pulses.

There are many reasons for excluding or avoiding animal protein. You may or may not be motivated by moral and ethical issues, but whatever your views in this respect, there are plenty of good medical indicators to consider in relation to animal protein and animal products. Along with your steak and chicken wings you will very likely be getting an unwanted dose of antibiotics, a dangerous collection of different hormones and a variety of unexpected toxic extras. Concentrations of many of the substances injected into animals or added to their food have proved to be potentially cancer-promoting and evidence shows that they can be passed on from the treated animal to the unsuspecting consumer. Until animal husbandry is radically reviewed, the undesirable chemical cocktails that all too often accompany meat would be reason alone to avoid it. Unfortunately, fish is not much safer. Increasing levels of water pollution have led to worryingly high deposits of mercury and other contaminants in fish.

But even if you found reliable sources of meat and fish that had been properly reared and farmed, it is still true that animal proteins are very hard to digest. Your body has to make a great effort to break it down, extract the nutrients from it and pass the resulting waste through the colon and out of the body. By all accounts this doesn't happen nearly quickly enough, with the result that the undigested byproducts of animal protein lie around in the large intestine for much, much longer than is good for us. This fact alone has been held responsible for a myriad of physical ailments ranging from constipation to cancer.

Another good reason for cutting out animal protein is that it is high in fat, and so too are the animal byproducts like butter, milk and cheese.

Low fat

Given the bombardment of information on this subject, it would be difficult not to know that most of us eat far too much fat with seriously unhealthy consequences. We are familiar with the link between high fat (in the form of cholesterol) and heart disease, but perhaps less aware of the link with cancer. Epidemiological studies show that where there is a high consumption of fat in the diet, there is a high level of cancer in the population. This is particularly true for hormone-related cancers like breast, uterine, ovarian and testicular.

Not only do we know that there is a connection between overconsumption of fat and the onset of cancer, but also it has been shown that reducing fat intake **after** the disease has developed can help to prevent it recurring. Knowing this makes it easier to be firm about replacing puddings, ice-creams and cheeses, tempting though they may be, with some of the exciting alternatives in the recipe section.

However, market forces being what they are, we are assaulted at every turn by exhortations from manufacturers claiming to offer a 'healthy low-fat alternative' to just about everything from butter to biscuits and this can be confusing. Don't be tempted or fooled by any of this. Many so-called 'substitutes' still contain fat – sometimes only an infinitesimally smaller amount than the 'real thing' – and, equally relevant, they are likely to be positively bristling with additives and E-numbers too numerous to name.

A healthy diet must contain a certain amount of fat and, in this nutritional scheme, the essential fatty acids come from a selection of nuts and seeds and from the careful use of olive oil and some other cold-pressed oils.

Whole and unprocessed

All too often the price of the process of 'refinement' is to diminish the nutritional value of food. When rice is polished, the husk is removed and thrown away or fed to animals. Lucky animals. The husk contains an abundance of vitamins and trace elements and the nutritional value of the rice is lessened without it. Much the same happens when wheat husk is separated from the grain in order to produce flour that can be milled to a fine, powdery whiteness. As a general rule, it is preferable to eat food that has not been interfered with too much. Not only does this mean that you are getting the maximum nutritional benefit from it, but it also means you are avoiding an unwanted dose of the many and various substances required to process a food into a product. Many of those tins and packets of ready-made gourmet recipes have lists of ingredients that sound rather alarming if considered in the context of optimum nutrition. Whether your goal is to stay well or to get well, you can't afford to waste energy. And your body will have to use a lot of energy in its efforts to sort out all the colourings, preservatives, flavour enhancers, solidifiers and so on that are an inevitable part of processing techniques.

This is a point well worth remembering in relation to stimulants like tea, coffee, sugar, salt and alcohol. Most of us consume far more than we should of some, if not all, of these. Such refined stimulants throw the body into a state of almost continuous physiological stress. This is because the essential task of checking and balancing the effects of these substances uses up enormous amounts of power, to say nothing of precious stores of vitamins and minerals as well. In its struggle to maintain homeostasis, the body is forced to use energy and resources that it needs for other functions. This is not just a pointless waste of time, it is positively dangerous. A perfect balance between sodium (salt) and potassium is an essential prerequisite for the healthy functioning of every cell in the body – something worth remembering if we have become attached to the idea of salty flavours. There are other, healthy, ways of creating savoury flavours, and sweet ones too. Read on!

Organically grown

Life is a lot easier now that most big supermarkets stock organically grown produce somewhere on their shelves. It is still likely to be more expensive than its more chemically encouraged commercial cousin, but think of all the money you're saving at the meat counter. There is now a high cultural awareness of the risks to human health from the excessive and extensive use of pesticides and fertilisers, some of which do enter the food chain and can create havoc. The use of nitrate is now carefully monitored and controlled, but it is still the base of many brands of fertiliser. Nitrate converts to nitrite, (which is frequently used as a preservative), and this in turn develops into nitrosamines. Nitrosamine is a potent carcinogen. Need I say more. This is tough, but true. Go organic if you can and when you can, but don't worry about it if you can't. It's impossible to control every mouthful of food you eat, or every lungful of air you breathe, or each sip of water you take. Do the best you can and then enjoy what you've done.

More raw

It may sound a bit cheeky for a cookery book to suggest that you eat your food raw, but on this diet it would be good to aim for a fifty/fifty balance between raw and cooked food. Raw food has the advantage of being the closest it can possibly be to its natural, growing state. Nothing has been boiled out of it, stirred into it, added to it, or taken from it. All the nutrients are there as nature intended and you are getting them first hand. This is as good as it gets. There is also another quality about raw food that is of vital significance. And I mean **vital**. The word 'vitamin' comes from 'vital-amine' and there is a school of thought that believes this **vital**ity is locked up with the enzymes present in raw food. Most of the enzymes are killed by the cooking process and therefore lost to us. Max Gerson – one of the giants of innovative medicine from

whose work comes much of our understanding of the role of diet in cancer – believed that enzymes were an absolutely essential part of any anticancer treatment. The enzymes are there for the taking, but they die quickly. Some – but only some – will be lost in the picking, transporting and packaging, and a few more are lost when you start chopping and grating, but whole, raw food is a marvellous source of vital, living, enzymes. So experiment and enjoy.

At first it will feel strange to be eating such a high percentage of your food in its raw state, so, if you're not used to this, introduce the change slowly. Make sure you eat a wide variety of fruit and vegetables so that you always enjoy this part of your diet. One quick and easy way to increase your consumption of raw fruit and vegetables is to juice them or puree them. A glass of fresh vegetable or fruit juice before a meal is a wonderful way to get the digestive enzymes livened up. It's true that a few more enzymes are lost in the process but the rewards are still terrific. There is a big section on salads and raw meals in this book which will suggest some new ideas and different possibilities.

Summary

- This is a diet that demands the least and gives the most.
- By avoiding food that is difficult to digest or contains harmful additives, you are saving energy and avoiding risk.
- By eating food that is healthy, vital and energising, you will feel better and be healthier.
- A high-protein diet full of fat, salt, sugar and additives (in other words a typical 'modern' diet) is stressful to the body, exhausts the immune system and is potentially lethal.
- This diet – rich in vegetable protein,

organically grown fruit and vegetables, low in fat, salt and sugar – is a positive enhancer of the immune system. The enzymes, energy and nutrients it contains will help the healthy stay healthy and the sick get well. Children, adults and elderly people will all benefit from it, so eat and live well!

Myths and legends

I would like to take just a moment to look at a few of the issues that are raised frequently in my teaching sessions and in the mail.

'I've been told that tomatoes can be bad for health.'

This belief comes from an old suspicion that all fruits and vegetables from the nightshade family are potentially poisonous. However, if we ruled out every member of this plant family we would be denied not just tomatoes, but aubergines, peppers and potatoes as well. Many doctors and nutritionists are well aware of this theory but they do not believe that it should be a cause for concern; tomatoes, potatoes, peppers and aubergines appear regularly in many cuisines. The people of the Mediterranean countries eat more of these vegetables than just about anyone else and they are enviably healthy, which suggests that we don't have too much to worry about. The only exception to this might be people who suffer from rheumatoid arthritis, who should take further advice.

Tomatoes also contain a carotenoid-lycopene (red pigment). Recent studies show that people with high levels of this in their blood are at much lower risk of developing various forms of cancer – particularly bladder, cervix and pancreas. More good news is that this vital ingredient is still present in pureed tomatoes so, although tomato puree could be described as a processed food, it is still recommended.

'If I'm not drinking milk then I must be deficient in calcium.'

Wrong. We can get calcium in the same way that the cows get it in the first place – 'by eating our greens'. A cup of cooked rhubarb contains more calcium than a cup of milk and a generous head of broccoli can claim the same, but first prize must go to the amazing poppy seed which boasts a staggering 1200mg per 100g. Other grains and seeds also contain calcium so there's plenty to be had, don't worry.

'I'm frightened I won't get enough protein if I can't eat meat or cheese.'

This begs the question of how much is enough since most people eat far more protein than they need or use, thus loading up and exhausting their digestive system. Protein consists of a chain of 22 amino-acids and just about all the beans, pulses (legumes) and nuts contain some, if not most, of these. By eating a selection of foods at every meal, you will certainly be getting all the protein you need. If you are ever in doubt, eat a few almonds or some tofu as well and stop worrying about it.

'There's no point in me ever starting this diet because I just have to have the occasional cup of tea/glass of wine/piece of wedding cake.'

Don't let this stop you. If you indulge in a few treats and lapse from time to time, you'll be just like the rest of us. You can't invalidate weeks of nourishment by throwing in a few mouthfuls of rubbish.

Reminders, hints and information

Fruit and vegetables

<u>Most important</u> – vegetables and fruit are the kings and queens of this diet. They should be fresh and organic whenever possible and form

the greater part of your intake. Eat lots of them – in salads and cooked in as great a variety of ways as you can find. Generally use them scrubbed rather than peeled. Enjoy them and keep looking for new ones to try.

Grains and pulses (legumes)

Less familiar for some people will be the grains, beans and seeds that form the next most important ingredient in this style of eating. Again buy organic when possible/affordable/available. There's

---

Cooking grains and pulses (legumes)

(Toasting rice or grains for 5 minutes in a dry pan before adding water will cut the cooking time by 10 minutes.)

For one cup dry:	add cups of water:	and cook for:
Whole brown rice	3 cups	1 hour
Whole wheat 'berries'	3 cups	2 hours
Buckwheat (kasha)	2 cups	15 minutes
Bulgar wheat	2 cups	15–20 minutes (soak, then steam)
Millet	3 cups	35–40 minutes
Cous cous	2 cups	15–20 minutes (soak, then steam)
Lentils (small red)	3 cups	35–40 minutes
Split peas or green lentils	3 cups	40–45 minutes
Mung beans	3 cups	35–40 minutes
Chick peas (garbanzos)	4 cups	THREE HOURS
Cannellini, flageolet, navy beans	3 cups	2 hours 30 minutes
Pinto beans	3 cups	2 hours 30 minutes
Butter beans (white lima)	2 cups	2 hours 30 minutes
Black-eye peas	3 cups	1 hour 30 minutes
Quinoa	2 cups	15 minutes (add grain to boiling water)

---

no need to go mad with these, especially if you're not used to eating them, just work them in gently. Unless you have a really big family, try buying a small amount of a wide variety because they don't keep their flavour or nutrients indefinitely. Some beans need soaking overnight and most take a long time to cook; none of them will ever be hurried. So, to allow for some creative spontaneity and the odd emergency, I advise keeping a few tins of cooked beans (organic if possible) in the cupboard. Better still, cook more than you need each time. Cooked beans store very well in plastic bags in the freezer. Small portions thaw quickly, but large amounts may take as long to defrost as they take to cook in the first place.

Fats and oils

Use cold-pressed oils for cooking and for dressings. Olive oil is delicious and is readily available. Healthfood stores often have cold-pressed sunflower oil which is also good. One or two of the recipes suggest using soya margarine; if you've ever tried making (or eating) pastry made entirely with olive oil you'll know why.

Flours

100% wholewheat organic flour is good for most dishes but rice, potato or maize flours are an excellent alternative if you have a gluten intolerance. In any case, they can be very useful for thickening sauces and in cakes and cookies. Pastry made with rice flour can be difficult to handle and it is worth experimenting with some of the many different alternatives like maize (polenta and cornmeal), potato flour, chick pea flour, gram flour (split peas) and – unbelievably – banana flour. If you aren't happy with your initial efforts to produce tasty pastry using 100% wholewheat flour, allow yourself to compromise by using part organic white flour.

Tofu

Tofu is now widely available. It is a highly nutritious food made from the milk produced by boiling ground soya beans. It is very low in fat and cholesterol and high in protein. It is very useful for both sweet and savoury dishes – everything from strawberry mousse to garlic mayonnaise.

Vinegar

Generally try to use cider vinegar (organic is best). It has a gentle alkaline effect on the stomach and digestive system.

I find it very handy to keep a jar of yellow or black mustard seeds soaking in cider vinegar or apple juice in a jar in the fridge as they give a lovely mellow taste to dressings and sauces.

Salt

One of the objectives of this diet is to reduce salt intake. Modern food processing techniques rely heavily on salt and have accustomed us to expect and anticipate a salty taste when we eat. This habit takes a bit of breaking, but it is only a habit and too much salt is incompatible with good health. The sodium in salt is readily available in a wholefood diet so there is no need to add more. If you are looking for more savoury flavours, try experimenting with some of these:

- tamari soy sauce
- shoyu soy sauce
- miso, fermented soya/rice barley
- vitamin R low-sodium spread (made by Mapletons)

- potassium-based salt substitute
- potassium-based baking powder
- low salt bouillon powder (Marigold make a good one)

Shoyu is a naturally aged and fermented soy sauce made from soya beans and wheat in almost equal proportions, plus some salt. Tamari is a similar product but it is generally fermented without the wheat. These two are pretty well interchangeable and most healthfood shops will stock them, but check the label for additives. Be careful too with soy sauce. I don't recommend the commercial supermarket brands of dark brown liquid known simply as 'soy sauce'. These are usually an unfermented preparation made from hydrolysed vegetable protein (HVP), syrup, caramel colouring, salt, often they contain huge amounts of monosodium glutamate.

Miso paste is another naturally fermented product made from soya beans and grains. There are several varieties because the different grains used create a range of flavours. It is usually made with brown rice or barley and, like tamari and shoyu, it contains salt. It's worth the search to find organic miso because it has a richer flavour. Best of all is miso fermented with the 'klebsiella' bacteria because it offers an extra source of the invaluable and elusive Vitamin B_{12}.

As you can see, all these products contain some salt so they can hardly be called 'substitutes'. However, small amounts go a long way and there will be an overall reduction in sodium levels, providing you don't use too much.

Sugar

'Pure, white and deadly, nothing but empty calories' – you've heard it all before. Refined sugar does you no good at all and, unfortunately, it can have a positively deleterious effect on the body as the digestive system struggles to deal with it. However, as with salt, we have all become subtly attached to the presence of sugar in a wide and surprising range of foods, so even people who claim not to have a sweet tooth may discover that they miss this flavour. Happily there are plenty of substitutes. To sweeten custards, cakes and puddings try organic apple concentrate (very, very sweet); other fruit syrups and concentrates are also available; maple syrup and date syrup are good too.

Malt extract

This is very useful for adding depth to the flavour of sauces and soups. Try adding a tablespoon 10 minutes before the end of the cooking time in a rich tomato sauce for pasta or in a vegetable casserole.

What you need to make the change

Making these changes in your diet should not require having to make drastic changes in your kitchen. None of these recipes require any complicated equipment, but you will find life is a lot easier if you have at least these few simple tools:

1 **A sharp knife** – the difference between pleasure and pain when preparing vegetables. Treat yourself to a good quality knife and remember to keep it sharpened. A blunt knife is dangerous as well as frustrating.
2 **A casserole pan** – 23–25cm square (9–10in) and 8–10cms (3–4in) deep is a good size. This will feed between four and six people with dishes like Creamy Golden Casserole. It should have a lid, be oven and flameproof and preferably be made of enamel (such as Le Creuset), glass, earthenware or stainless steel.

3 **A few nice, friendly saucepans.** Some pots just aren't helpful and it's a shame if you do well but your pans let you down. Heavy bottoms cook food evenly without sticking or burning. Stainless steel and enamel are good and easy to clean.
4 **A deep roasting tray** about 23 x 27cms (9 x 12in) square.
5 **A loose bottom metal flan case** 2.5 x 4cms (1 x 2in) deep.
6 **Some glass jars with lids** for storing beans and seeds. (Nuts keep their flavour better in the fridge.)
7 **A good, simple grater.**
8 **An electric blender** with a goblet or an electric hand blender.
9 **A food processor** (such as Magimix).

As you gain confidence, you will find that you can treat these recipes simply as ideas. They may have started out as my ideas, but you can soon make them your own by adding, omitting, or adapting according to personal preferences. The instructions and ingredients have been tested to give a good result, but after a while you won't need to follow them teaspoon by teaspoon; enjoy yourself and allow yourself to be creative.

A note about portion sizes

Most of my recipes are about the right quantity to feed four hungry people or as a side dish or starter for six.

Index of Recipes

Hot Vegetable Dishes

Soups and Savoury Sauces

Bright Red Pepper (Bell Pepper) Sauce

*Makes about 600 ml
(1 pint/2½ cups)*

*2 garlic cloves (optional)
1 medium onion, chopped
3 red peppers (bell peppers),
    chopped
3 tablespoons olive oil
2 teaspoons low-salt stock
    (bouillon) powder
2 teaspoons tomato purée
    (tomato paste)
pinch of paprika
300 ml (½ pint/1 cup) water*

Soften the vegetables a little in the oil. Add the
remaining ingredients, stirring after each addition,
adding the water last. Reduce the heat, cover
and cook gently until the peppers are very soft,
about 30 minutes.
Let cool a little and whizz until smooth in
the blender.

*This sauce is not only delicious but always looks
dramatic and impressive. It's wonderful with grains or
pasta or served in a little pool beside Parsnip Dabs
(see page 86). Also, try whizzing a handful of fresh basil
leaves into it for a taste explosion!*

Courgette (Zucchini) and Tarragon Soup

Serves 4–6

---

1 large onion, roughly chopped
3 tablespoons olive oil
6 or 8 medium courgettes
    (zucchini) (you need about
    1 kg/2¼ lbs), roughly chopped
2 tablespoons dried or fresh
    tarragon leaves

Sauté the onion in the oil gently until soft, but do not let it go brown. Add the courgettes (zucchini) and herbs and stir.

---

600 ml (1 pint/2 cups) soya milk
600 ml (1 pint/2 cups) vegetable
    stock or water
2 teaspoons low-salt stock
    (bouillon) powder (optional)
1 teaspoon ground black pepper

Add these to the other ingredients, bring to the boil and simmer gently for 20 minutes. Then blend in a blender until smooth.

This is a light, delicious soup that is quick to prepare. If you want it a bit heartier in the autumn, add a couple of chopped potatoes with the onions. If it's the middle of summer, add a handful of fresh mint at the blending stage and serve it well chilled.

Creamed Garlic Sauce

Makes about 600 ml
(1 pint/2½ cups)

---

1 medium potato, finely chopped
10 garlic cloves, peeled
600 ml (1 pint/2 cups) soya milk
pinch of dried thyme
pinch of ground nutmeg
pinch of ground black pepper
1 teaspoon tamari (optional)

Bring everything gently to the boil. Cover, reduce
the heat and cook very gently for 35 minutes, or
until the potato and garlic break up when prodded
with a fork.
Whizz until smooth in a blender or push through
a mouli or strainer.

---

*Try this sauce poured over pasta with cooked vegetables
and baked for 15 minutes to brown or with stuffed
vegetables or simply with steamed vegetables and brown
rice.*

Creamy Cauliflower Soup

Serves 4–6

---

2 medium potatoes, scrubbed and
    chopped (if you want a really
    smooth soup, peel them first)
600 ml (1 pint/2 cups) soya milk
600 ml (1 pint/2 cups) vegetable
    stock or water
4 teaspoons low-salt stock
    (bouillon) powder

Simmer together gently, covered, in a large pan until
the potatoes are really soft.

---

1 medium cauliflower, cut into
    small pieces, stalks and small
    leaves too
handful of fresh mint leaves or
    2 teaspoons dried mint
1 teaspoon ground nutmeg
1 teaspoon ground black pepper
4 sprigs of fresh mint, to garnish

Add these ingredients to the pan and simmer,
uncovered, for approximately 20 minutes, until
the cauliflower is tender.
Let cool slightly and blend until smooth – not for too
long or the potatoes can become gluey. Serve with a
sprig of mint on each bowl.

Creamy Curry Sauce

*Makes about 1.2 litres
2 pints/5 cups)*

2 tablespoons cold-pressed sunflower oil 1 onion, finely chopped	Sauté gently together until the onion is soft but has not browned
1 teaspoon cumin 1 teaspoon ground coriander 1 teaspoon turmeric 1 teaspoon paprika	Add to the onion, cook and stir over a low heat for 2 minutes.
2 tablespoons gram or wholemeal (wholewheat) flour	Remove the pan from the heat while you stir in the flour. Mix well.
350 g (12 oz/1½ cups silken or fresh tofu 350 ml (⅔ pint/1½ cups) water juice of 2 lemons 3 tablespoons tamari 300 ml (½ pint/1 cup) soya milk	Whizz together in a blender and stir slowly into the spicy mixture in the pan. Return the pan to a gentle heat and cook, stirring all the time, for 4–5 minutes until the sauce has thickened.

Use as a side sauce or pour over cooked vegetables and oven bake until golden and bubbling, for example cauliflower, broccoli, onions, potatoes, carrots, squash, courgettes (zucchini) or parsnips – all taste great.

Fresh Corn Chowder

Serves 4–6

---

3 tablespoons olive or sunflower oil 2 medium onions, finely chopped	Sauté together in a large pan over a low heat for 8 minutes.

---

4 fresh corn cobs
1 potato, finely chopped
600 ml (1 pint/2 cups) soya milk
600 ml (1 pint/2 cups) water or
    vegetable stock
2 teaspoons low-salt stock
    (bouillon) powder
1 teaspoon ground black pepper
½ teaspoon ground nutmeg
	Discard the leaves and hairy bits of the corn cobs. For each, stand the fat end firmly on a large chopping board, hold the pointed end and use a sharp knife to cut straight down behind the kernels to remove them from the cob.
	Stir the corn and the rest of the ingredients into the onion mixture and gently bring to the boil.
	Simmer gently for 35 minutes.
	Remove from the heat and let cool slightly. Blend half the soup in a blender and return to the pan. Heat gently again and serve.

If you blend the whole lot until smooth, this also becomes a versatile sauce for pouring over other cooked vegetables. You can also layer it with slices of parboiled potatoes, bake in a 190°C/375°F/gas 5 oven for 35–40 minutes and then you'll have a tasty lunch dish to serve with a salad.

Good All Round Tomato Sauce

*Makes about 1.2 litres
(2 pints/5 cups)*

---

*4 tablespoons olive oil
2 onions, finely chopped
1 teaspoon dried oregano
1 teaspoon dried basil
1 teaspoon fennel seeds (optional)
4 garlic cloves, sliced
1 teaspoon ground black pepper*

Soften together in good, heavy based saucepan.

---

*100 g (4 oz/½ cup) tomato purée
   (tomato paste)
1 carrot, grated
1 small red or green pepper, finely
   chopped
400 g (14 oz/2 cups) chopped fresh
   or canned tomatoes
1 tablespoon tamari
300 ml (½ pint/⅓ cup) water
1 tablespoon dark malt extract*

Stir the tomato purée (tomato paste) into the softened onion over a gentle heat for 3–4 minutes, then add the rest of the ingredients. Stir well, lower the heat and simmer for 25–30 minutes. Cook a little longer if you like it a bit thicker.

Great on any kind of pasta or vegetables. Left to reduce and thicken, it's a good pizza topping.

Good Gravy

Makes about 900 ml
(1½ pints/3¾ cups)

---

4 tablespoons cornflour
   (cornstarch) or arrowroot or rice
   flour or potato flour
300 ml (½ pint/1 cup) apple juice
600 ml (1 pint/2 cups) water or
   vegetable stock
2 teaspoons low-salt stock
   (bouillon) powder
4 tablespoons tamari

Blend the flour to a smooth paste with a few spoon-fuls of water. Bring everything else to a rolling boil and, after 3–4 minutes, add the paste and stir well while it returns to the boil.

Serve anytime you need a good savoury gravy, say with a nut roast or vegetable pie. A splash of organic red wine or a spoonful of malt extract adds an extra something, too! Or use 250 ml (8 fl oz/1 cup) of soya milk in place of this amount of the water or vegetable stock to make it creamy.

Lightly Spicy Carrot and Pumpkin Soup

Serves 4–6

---

2 tablespoons olive or sunflower oil
1 teaspoon black mustard seeds
1 teaspoon cumin seeds
stick of cinnamon or pinch of
  ground cinnamon
1 onion, finely chopped
1 teaspoon turmeric
1 bay leaf

Heat the oil in a large pan, add the mustard seeds and let them pop about for a few seconds (you might need to put the lid on). Add the other ingredients and sauté until the onion softens.

---

450 g (1 lb/2 cups) pumpkin or
  other golden-fleshed squash,
  peeled and chopped small
450 g (1lb/2 cups) carrots,
  scrubbed and chopped small
1 litre (1¾ pints/4 cups) water or
  ½ water, ½ apple juice

Stir the vegetables into the spicy onions. Add the liquid, stir, cover and simmer for about 35 minutes, or until the carrots are soft.

---

25 g (1 oz) piece of fresh root
  ginger, grated with the skin on
2 teaspoons tamari

Take the pan off the heat. Put the grated ginger in the palm of your hand and squeeze hard – watch the precious juice drip into the soup – then discard the pulp. Stir in the tamari and serve.

I like this soup with the bits in, but if you like your soup smooth, just remove the cinnamon stick and bay leaf and process in a blender.
This soup is lovely with fresh coriander (cilantro) leaves on top.

Mustard Sauce for Grilled (Broiled) Vegetables

Makes sufficient to coat vegetables for 2 as a main course

2 tablespoons yellow mustard
    seeds, soaked overnight in cider
    vinegar
2 tablespoons clear honey
2 tablespoons tamari
1 tablespoon olive oil
ground black pepper, to taste

Whizz together in a blender.

Spoon or spread this sauce on vegetables and grill (broil) for a tasty snack or side dish. Try it on the following, for example:

- *halved tomatoes – 10 minutes*
- *thin slices of aubergine (eggplant)
    – 10 minutes each side*
- *thin slices of courgette (zucchini)
    – 10 minutes each side*
- *onion wedges
    – 15 minutes each side*
- *whole cooked corn cobs
    – 10 minutes turning during cooking*
- *parboiled slices of potato
    – 5 minutes each side*
- *parboiled slices of parsnip
    – 5 minutes each side*
- *thick slices of fresh tofu
    – 5 minutes each side*

Nearly Raw Cream of Vegetable Soup

Serves 4–6

---

1 litre (1¾ pints/4 cups) organic
  soya milk
2 tomatoes, chopped
2 carrots, chopped
2 celery sticks, chopped
handful of fresh parsley (and/or
  other fresh herbs)
½ small cauliflower, chopped
2 teaspoons low-salt yeast extract
  (e.g. Vitam R)
½ teaspoon ground black
  pepper
½ teaspoon nutmeg

Blend until smooth in a blender.

---

2 onions, finely chopped
50 g (2 oz/¼cup) soya margarine

Soften the onion gently with the margarine in a heavy based pan, but don't let them brown. Add the cream of vegetables and simmer very gently for 10–15 minutes.

The soup looks good served sprinkled with chopped green herbs.

Parsnip and Brown Rice Soup

Serves 4–6

3 medium parsnips, scrubbed and
    chopped small
1 medium onion, chopped
2 tablespoons olive oil
1 teaspoon cumin seeds
1 litre (2 pints/4 cups) water
120 ml (4 fl oz/½ cup) tamari
2 bay leaves

Place all the ingredients in a heavy based pan,
bring to the boil, then reduce the heat and simmer
for about 35 minutes, until the parsnips are
very tender.

350 g (12 oz/2 cups) cooked brown
    rice i.e. 1 cup raw (see page 13
    for cooking time)
2 tablespoons miso

Stir into soup.

*The soup is ready to serve at this point, but it is even
more delicious if you blend half or two-thirds of the soup
and return to the pan, reheat it and serve with a little
grated red apple sprinkled on top.*

Sauce Chinoise for
Raw Vegetables

*Makes about 300 ml
(½ pint/scant 2 cups)*

*2 tablespoons tamari
2 teaspoons clear honey
3 tablespoons cider vinegar
2 tablespoons miso
½ teaspoon Chinese five spice
   powder
2 tablespoons roasted sesame oil
4 tablespoons sunflower oil*

Whisk together until blended.

Try this over a salad of shredded Chinese leaves, sliced spring onions (scallions), cucumber strips and fresh coriander (cilantro) sprigs or with grated broccoli and beansprouts.

Hot and Cold Salads

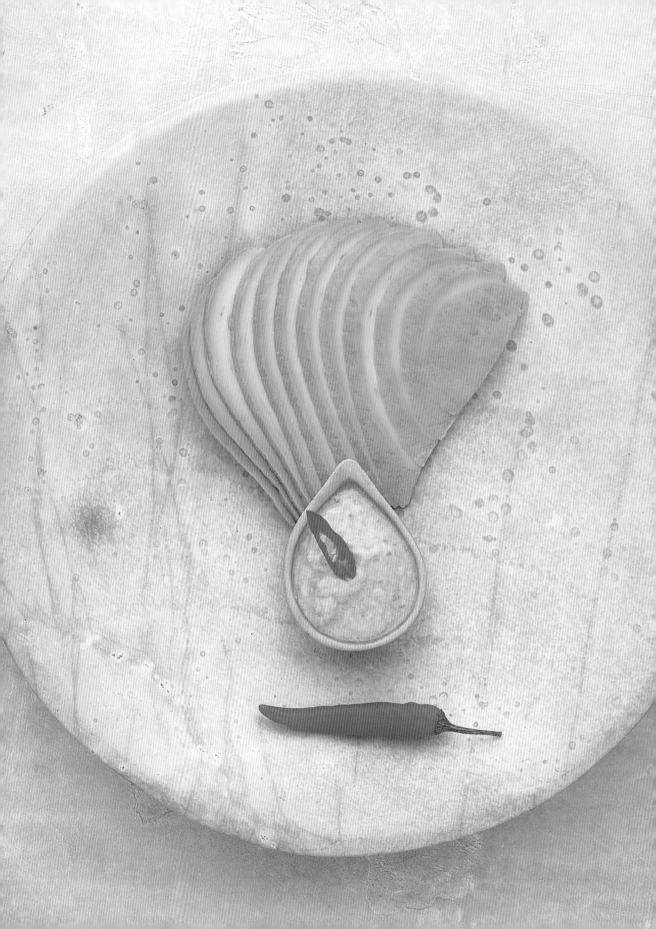

Avocados with Garlic Cream Dressing

Serves 4

---

*100 g (4 oz/ ½ cup) fresh or silken
   tofu*
2 tasty, ripe tomatoes
*2 garlic cloves, peeled and
   chopped*
*1 small, mild onion or shallot,
   grated*
1 teaspoon tamari
¼ teaspoon ground black pepper

Mix in a blender until smooth. Chill.

---

2 ripe avocados, peeled and sliced
grating of nutmeg

Arrange the avocado slices on individual plates
and serve with the Garlic Cream Dressing and a
grating of nutmeg.

Broccoli, Macadamia and Garlic Salad

Serves 4–6

---

approximately 75 g (3 oz/½ cup)
   cooked chickpeas
   (garbanzos)
2 tablespoons olive oil
85 ml (3 fl oz/scant ½ cup) cider
   vinegar
2 garlic cloves
½ teaspoon ground black pepper

Combine for a few seconds in a blender until the mixture is the consistency of single (light) cream. Add a little water or lemon juice if it's a bit thick.

---

2 or 3 fresh firm heads of broccoli,
   divided into florets and sliced
   from stem to top, very thinly
150 g (5 oz/1 cup) macadamia
   nuts, sliced, or 65 g
   (2½ oz/ ½ cup) toasted
   pine nuts

Pile the broccoli onto a plate or in a shallow bowl. Scatter with the nuts and drizzle the dressing over the top.

This is one of those recipes where having a few leftover cooked chickpeas (garbanzos) in the refrigerator or freezer means you can make a very quick tasty meal at the last minute.

Creamy Sweet Potato Salad

Serves 4–6

---

3 medium sweet potatoes or
  ordinary potatoes, if you like,
  cooked whole in their skins then
  cubed
1 green pepper (bell pepper), finely
  chopped
2 celery sticks, with leaves, finely
  chopped
3 spring onions (scallions), thinly
  sliced
75 g (3 oz/½ cup) chopped
  hazelnuts
½ walnut-size piece of fresh
  ginger, peeled and finely grated
  or ½ teaspoon dried ginger
  powder

Gently mix together.

---

100 g (4 oz/½ cup) silken or fresh
  tofu
2 tablespoons cold-pressed oil
2 tablespoons cider vinegar
1 tablespoon lemon juice
1 tablespoon tamari
1 tablespoon yellow mustard seeds
  soaked in apple juice (optional)
2 tablespoons hazelnuts, toasted,
  to garnish
3 or 4 sprigs of celery leaves,
  to garnish

Give the tofu a quick whizz in a food processor, then add the other ingredients. The mixture should be the consistency of a thick mayonnaise. Add a little water to keep it moving if it gets too thick.
Fold the tofu mayonnaise into the vegetables and chill for 1 hour. Serve with some toasted hazelnuts or celery leaves on top.

Mediterranean
Rice Salad

Serves 4–6

---

*350 g (12 oz/2 cups) cooked brown
   rice i.e. 1 cup raw (see page 13
   for cooking time)*
*20 black olives, stoned (pitted) and
   halved*
4 ripe tomatoes, chopped
kernels cut from 2 cooked corn cobs
handful of fresh basil, chopped
3 garlic cloves, crushed
3 tablespoons olive oil
2 tablespoons tamari
*juice and zest (grated peel) of
   1 lemon*
*1 red or green pepper (bell pepper),
   finely chopped*

Mix gently, then set to one side, covered, for 1 hour
before serving.

Middle Eastern
Rice Salad

Serves 4–6

---

*350 g (12 oz/2 cups) cooked brown
   rice i.e. 1 cup raw (see page 13
   for cooking time)*
6 chopped dates, fresh or dried
3 tablespoons toasted cashew nuts
*4 spring onions (scallions), finely
   sliced*
2 tablespoons tamari
1 teaspoon toasted fennel seeds
1 teaspoon toasted cumin seeds
juice of 1 juicy lemon
3 tablespoons olive oil

Gently mix together and set to one side to 'develop'
for about 30 minutes.

Oriental Aubergine (Eggplant) Salad

Serves 4–6
Oven: 240°C/475°F/gas 9

85 ml (3 fl oz/scant ½ cup) olive
    oil
2 aubergines (eggplants) cut into
    approximately 1.25-cm (½-in)
    thick slices
2 red or white onions, thinly sliced
ground black pepper

Generously oil a baking sheet and spread a single layer of aubergine (eggplant) slices on it. Cover with a layer of onion and a sprinkling of oil and black pepper. (You may need to use 2 baking sheets or cook them in two batches.) Bake in the oven for about 40 minutes. Cool and chop roughly.

2 tablespoons fresh coriander
    (cilantro), chopped
2 tablespoons fresh dill or fennel
    leaves chopped
splash of cider vinegar
squeeze of lemon juice

Stir into the aubergines (eggplant). Chill and serve.

Nice as an hors d'oeuvre with hot garlic bread or piled on to small crisp lettuce leaves.

Salad Suedoise

Serves 4–6

---

4 tablespoons olive oil
4 tablespoons cider vinegar
2 teaspoons yellow mustard seeds,
    soaked overnight in apple juice
    or cider vinegar
1 teaspoon fresh or dried dill, finely
    chopped
1 tablespoon light tahini
1 tablespoon tamari
1 teaspoon ground black pepper

Mix together in a blender until smooth.

---

4 medium courgettes (zucchini),
    grated
2 apples, grated
2 carrots, grated
4 celery sticks, finely chopped
1 small bulb fennel, finely sliced
    (optional)

Gently fold into the dressing and serve.

This dressing also works well with grated cauliflower and carrots, or with cold, cooked potatoes and butter (lima) beans.

Scrumptious Tabbouleh

Serves 4–6

---

175 g (6 oz/1 cup) bulgar (cracked wheat) or couscous, soaked in cold water to cover for 2–2½ hours

Tip into a sieve or colander lined with a clean cloth, then twist the cloth around wheat and squeeze to extract all the moisture.

---

100 g (4 oz/1 cup) onion, very finely chopped

Turn the wheat into a large bowl and knead in the onion with your hand for a couple of minutes.

---

75 g (3 oz/1½ cups) parsley, finely chopped
25 g (1 oz/½ cup) fresh mint, finely chopped
2 tomatoes, finely chopped
½ cucumber, finely chopped
½ teaspoon ground black pepper
4 tablespoons olive oil
4 tablespoons lemon juice

Mix gently and thoroughly into the wheat mixture and chill for 1 hour.

Pile onto a bed of cos (or crisp) lettuce. Garnish with olives, pine nuts or nasturtium leaves and flowers if you have some.

If at the chilling stage you press the mixture down well into an oiled bowl or simple jelly mould, it will keep its shape when inverted onto a serving plate and given a firm tap, and looks very impressive served with aubergines (eggplant) and salsa verde.

Slaw Chinoise

Serves 4–6

---

1 small white cabbage, really finely
   shredded
100 g (4 oz/2 cups) shredded
   Chinese leaves
2 bunches spring onions
   (scallions), sliced
1 sweet apple, cut into fine strips or
   grated
50 g (2 oz/1 cup) mung bean
   sprouts

Mix together.

---

2 tablespoons whole almonds
2 tablespoons sesame seeds

Toast gently in dry pan (keep the lid handy so that
the sesame seeds do not jump out all over the
cooker). Cool and chop.

---

2 tablespoons sunflower oil
1 teaspoon roasted sesame oil
2 tablespoons cider vinegar
1 generous teaspoon clear honey
½ teaspoon ground black pepper
2 teaspoons tamari

Blend together and gently mix with the vegetables
and toasted nuts.

Spinach and Sunflower Seed Salad

Serves 4–6

---

150 ml (¼ pint/½ cup) cider
   vinegar
2 tablespoons lemon juice
100 g (4 oz/½ cup) dried
   apricots

Bring the vinegar just to the boil in a small pan, remove from the heat and add the lemon juice and apricots. Leave to soak for about 30 minutes, stirring occasionally. Then, drain over a bowl, reserving the juice. Chop the apricots.

---

150 g (5 oz/1 cup) sunflower seeds
2 tablespoons tamari

Put the seeds in a heavy, dry frying pan and stir gently over medium heat until just turning golden. Remove from the heat and quickly mix in the tamari – it will sizzle a lot and go sticky. Then, straight away, pour the mixture from the pan onto a cool plate or greaseproof paper (wax paper).

---

750 g (1½ lbs) young leaf
   spinach, torn into bite-size
   pieces

Put the spinach into a serving bowl and add the chopped apricots.

---

2 tablespoons olive oil
reserved juice from the apricots
1 teaspoon coarsely ground black
   pepper

Whisk together. Add to the spinach, apricots and sunflower seeds. Combine gently and serve.

Shredded red-skinned apple looks very pretty in this. Sunflower seeds prepared like this keep very well in an airtight jar and are useful for sprinkling and snacking.

Sweetie Beetie Salad

Serves 4–6

---

4 medium beetroots (beets), peeled
    and grated (cooked is good, but
    raw is best)
2 tablespoons sugar-free
    marmalade (orange preserve)
2 tablespoons grated fresh or
    dessicated coconut soaked in
    2 tablespoons soya milk for
    10 minutes
juice and grated rind (zest) of ½
    lemon
2 tablespoons currants
1 teaspoon cider vinegar
1 teaspoon miso mixed to smooth
    paste with 2 teaspoons warm
    water

Mix everything together and chill for 2 hours or so, to let the flavours melt together deliciously.

If you have any left, whizz it in the blender to make a spectacular dressing for sliced avoacdo or cold cooked potates (you may need to add a little water and/or cider vinegar to get the right consistency).

Tunisian-style Carrot Salad

Serves 4–6

---

85 ml (3 fl oz/scant ½ cup) oil
2 garlic cloves, very thinly sliced
450 g (1 lb) carrots, scrubbed and
    cut into thin strips

Heat the oil and toss in the carrots and garlic.
Let sizzle for 2 minutes. Reduce the heat, cover
and cook for 3–5 minutes more.

---

2 tablespoons cider vinegar
4 spring onions (scallions),
    sliced
½ teaspoon ground cloves
½ teaspoon ground cumin seeds
½ teaspoon paprika
1 teaspoon tamari

Add these to the pan in this order. Stir well, then
remove from the heat.

---

2 tablespoons chopped fresh mint
a few sprigs of mint, to garnish

Add to the carrots. Transfer to a bowl and chill before
serving, garnished with sprigs of mint.

Warm Cauliflower Salad

Serves 4–6

---

1 cauliflower, divided into florets, stalk and tiny leaves shredded

Cook in boiling water for 7 minutes, drain and put into a warm serving bowl.

---

juice of 1 lemon
2 teaspoons cider vinegar
2 tablespoons chopped fresh parsley
1 tablespoon chopped fresh mint
1 tablespoon light tahini
1 teaspoon ground black pepper

Whisk together.
Pour over the warm cauliflower and serve at once.

This dish looks pretty decorated with mint sprigs, a trail of light tahini and a few toasted walnuts, if you have them.

Warm Red Cabbage Salad with Watercress and Toasted Pecans

Serves 4–6

---

*1 small red cabbage, very finely
    shredded*
*2 small red onions, finely sliced
    and pulled into rings*
50 g (2 oz/1 cup) watercress

Mix together gently and arrange on
individual serving plates.

---

*50 g (2 oz/½ cup) pecans or
    walnuts*
2 tablespoons olive oil
1 small onion, very finely chopped
2 tablespoons orange juice
*1 teaspoon finely grated orange
    rind (peel)*
1 tablespoon cider vinegar

Sauté the nuts in half the oil until they are just
turning golden. Remove with slotted spoon and
share out over the prepared salads.
Add the onion and remaining oil to the pan and
stir over quite a high heat for a minute or two. Add
the orange juice, boil for a minute, then stir in the
other ingredients and heat through briefly. Pour
over the salads and serve immediately.

Warm Salad of Mixed Peppers and Tofu

Serves 4–6
Oven: 200°C/375°F/gas 6

---

6 peppers (bell peppers) of any
   mixed colours, very finely
   shredded
8 garlic cloves, chopped
4 tablespoons olive oil
5 tablespoons cider vinegar, plus
   extra for sprinkling
100 g (4 oz/½cup) tomato purée
   (tomato paste)
1 tablespoon tamari
1 tablespoon clear honey
1 teaspoon ground black pepper
1 teaspoon dried oregano
225 g (8 oz/1 cup) tofu, cut into
   thin strips
handful fresh basil leaves, chopped,
   plus a little extra for sprinkling

Gently combine all the ingredients and place on a roasting dish. Bake for 45–50 minutes, until the salad is starting to crisp and brown in places.

---

275 g (10 oz/4 cups) mixed small
   salad leaves, e.g. rocket
   (arugula), frisee (curly endive),
   spinach, radiccio

Divide between individual serving plates and top with the warm peppers. Sprinkle with a little more vinegar and fresh basil before serving.

Dressings, Dips and Spreads

Tomato and Coriander (Cilantro) Salsa

*Makes about 450 ml
(¾ pint/scant 2 cups)*

3 large, ripe tomatoes
1 onion or 6 spring onions
   (scallions)
2 garlic cloves
50 g (2 oz/1 cup) fresh coriander
   (cilantro) leaves
½ teaspoon ground black pepper
hot chilli pepper

Finely chop and mix all the ingredients together or whizz for a couple of seconds in a blender or food processor. (If you use a machine, start with the onions, then add the rest and process with short pulses or you'll risk ending up with a soup rather than a salsa!)

There are many varieties of salsa – which is somewhere between a salad and a sauce. This one is just as good with parsley or basil instead of the coriander (cilantro).

Carrot Mayonnaise Sauce

Makes about 600 ml
  (1 pint/2½ cups)

---

3 tablespoons olive oil
3 tablespoons cider vinegar
2 large carrots, chopped
175 (6 oz/1 cup) fresh tofu
2 tablespoons yellow mustard
  seeds, soaked overnight in cider
  vinegar
1 teaspoon ground black pepper
2 tablespoons miso

Blend the olive oil, vinegar and carrots until smooth, adding a little water to keep it moving if needed, then add the remaining ingredients and continue to blend. Stop and scrape down the sides a couple of times to make sure there are no lumps.

Creamy Avocado Dressing

Makes about 600 ml
  (1 pint/2½ cups)

---

2 ripe avocados, peeled and stone
  (pit) removed
300 ml (½ pint/⅓ cup) soya milk
1 tablespoon tamari
juice of 1 lemon
pinch of paprika
1 teaspoon light tahini
pinch of ground black pepper

Blend until smooth.

Creamy Mint Dressing

Makes about 600 ml
(1 pint/2½ cups)

---

4 tablespoons light tahini
2 teaspoons yellow mustard seeds,
soaked overnight in cider
vinegar
150 ml (¼ pint/½ cup) sunflower oil
150 ml (¼ pint/½ cup) cider
vinegar
15 g (½ oz/1 cup) fresh mint leaves
or 3 teaspoons dried mint
1 teaspoon ground black pepper
1 teaspoon tamari

Whizz until smooth in a blender.
Add a little water if it seems too thick to mix well.

Delicious poured over any crispy lettuce, such as cos,
romaine or little gem; or try it with loads of chopped
cucumber and/or onion to make a dairy-free raita to go
with Indian-style dishes.

Cucumber in Rich Walnut Sauce

Serves 4–6

---

*2 cucumbers cut into 2.5-cm (1-in)
   cubes.*

---

2 garlic cloves
1 tablespoon tamari
*15 g (½ oz/½ cup) fresh basil
   leaves or 1 teaspoon dried basil*
*100 g (4 oz/1 generous cup)
   walnuts*
3 tablespoons cider vinegar
juice of 1 lemon
25 g (1 oz/½ cup) chopped parsley
4–5 mint leaves
½ teaspoon ground black pepper
200 ml (⅓ pint/½ cup) olive oil

Whizz until smooth in a blender.
Pour over the cucumber. Serve immediately.

This makes a good dip, too. Cut cucumber, carrots and celery into 5-cm (2-in) sticks and serve with a small bowl of Rich Walnut Sauce. If you like a bit of a 'kick', you could add a small fresh green chilli pepper to the sauce. It's lovely with small crisp lettuce leaves, too.

Fresh Tomato and Basil Dressing

Makes about 300 ml
(½ pint/1¼ cups)

2 large, fresh, ripe tomatoes
2 tablespoons olive oil
1 tablespoon cider vinegar
generous handful of fresh basil
    leaves

Whizz in a blender until smooth.

Wonderful on cooked or raw vegetables. Add a chopped red pepper (bell pepper) for extra zing!

Orange and Sesame Dressing

Makes about 300 ml
(½ pint/1¼ cups)

zest (finely grated rind) of 1 large
    orange, the segments chopped
1 tablespoon cider vinegar
1 tablespoon tamari
1 teaspoon toasted sesame oil
1 teaspoon sesame seeds
2 tablespoons olive oil

Whizz together in a blender.

Delicious on a mixture of finely shredded red and green cabbage, with sultanas and almonds.

Lemon and Cumin Dressing

Makes about 300 ml
(½ pint/1¼ cups)

juice and zest (finely grated rind)
*   of 2 lemons*
1 large, ripe tomato
2 garlic cloves
2 teaspoons cumin seeds, lightly
*   toasted in a dry pan*
1 teaspoon tamari
pinch of paprika
2 tablespoons olive oil
1 teaspoon clear honey
1 teaspoon ground black pepper

Whizz together in a blender.

Lovely for a grain salad – try it poured over cooked rice, couscous, wheat berries or bulgar. Chill before adding your choice of chopped or grated raw vegetables.

Parsley Vinaigrette

Makes about 600 ml
  (1 pint/2½ cups)

---

150 ml (¼ pint/½ cup) olive oil
4 tablespoons cider vinegar
2 tablespoons tamari
1 teaspoon light tahini
zest (finely grated rind) of 1 lemon
50 g (2 oz/1 cup) fresh parsley

Whizz for a couple of minutes in a blender.

Vary this by using other herbs: basil is heavenly; mint or tarragon are good variations, too; or try a mixture with (or without) a clove of garlic.

Savoury Spread for Sandwiches or Toast

Makes about 600 ml
(1 pint/2½ cups)

250 ml (8 fl oz/1 cup) light tahini
300 ml (½ pint/1 cup) water
120 ml (4 fl oz/½ cup) tamari
1 tablespoon cider vinegar or
   lemon juice

Blend until thick and smooth.
Keeps well in the fridge.

*This spread is tasty, tangy and extremely versatile.
Lovely on hot toast or in a brown bread sandwich with
cucumber or sliced tomatoes. There are endless variations and I'm sure you will discover your own favourites,
but here are some options you might like to try.*
Add to the spread one of the following:

3 finely chopped tomatoes
2 tablespoons miso
50 g (2 oz/⅓ cup) fresh tofu
handful of chopped fresh basil
handful of chopped fresh mint
clove garlic, crushed (minced)
small onion, chopped
4 spring onions (scallions), chopped
100g (4 oz/½ cup) mashed, cooked beans.

Spicy Bean Paté

Serves 6

225 g (10 oz/1½ cups) pinto or aduki beans, soaked overnight *4 garlic cloves, peeled*	Cook the beans with the garlic in water until the beans are very soft. When cooked, mash with a fork or whizz in a blender.
1 large onion, finely chopped *2 garlic cloves, crushed (minced)* *1 red or green pepper (bell pepper), finely chopped* *2 tablespoons olive oil* *1 teaspoon ground cumin* *1 teaspoon paprika* *2 teaspoons tamari*	Sauté the vegetables in the oil over a gentle heat until soft. Stir in the spices. Fry another few minutes. Add the tamari. Stir the vegetable mixture into the beans and press into 6 ramekin pots or a bowl. Cool.
	Serve with hot bread as a first course or chill and use as a delicious sandwich filling.

Sunflower Spread for Sandwiches or Toast

Makes about 600 ml
(1 pint/2½ cups)

---

200 g (8 oz/1 cup) cooked green
split peas, drained and cooled,
i.e. 1 cup dried (see page 13
for cooking time)
1 generous tablespoon olive oil
100 g (4 oz/1 cup) toasted
sunflower seeds
3 tablespoons tamari (optional)
½ teaspoon ground black pepper
2 tablespoons lemon juice
½ teaspoon ground coriander

Grind the sunflower seeds in a food processor.
Add the other ingredients and whizz briefly to
blend the mixture until you have a coarse pâté
(or continue if you prefer a smooth texture).

You can vary this by adding a chopped and sautéed
onion. Fresh root ginger is also very good. Simply peel
and chop a 2.5-cm (1-in) piece, sauté it with a chopped
onion and add it to the mixture and whizz with the other
ingredients.

Tofu Mayonnaise

Makes about 600 ml
   (1 pint/2½ cups)

4 tablespoons lemon juice or cider
   vinegar
225 g (8 oz/1 cup) fresh organic or
   silken tofu
2 tablespoons olive oil
1 tablespoon tamari or shoyu
½ teaspoon ground black pepper
2–3 tablespoons water

Whizz together until smooth in a blender.

*There are many variations on this theme and I'm sure
you will find your own favourites, but here are just a few
to get you going.*

Oriental

Add
   1 teaspoon dark miso
   3 teaspoons spring onion (scallions), very finely
   chopped
   2 teaspoons finely grated fresh root ginger
   pinch of Chinese five spice powder

French

Add
   2 tablespoons yellow mustard seeds, soaked in cider
   vinegar and blended until smooth
   2 garlic cloves, crushed (minced)
   pinch of mixed dried herbs

Piquant

Add
   1 whole ripe tomato – liquidized
   ½ teaspoon paprika
   1 teaspoon clear honey
   2 teaspoons cider vinegar
   pinch dried oregano

Russian

Add

> *juice and zest (finely grated peel) of 1 lemon*
> *25 g (1 oz/½ cup) chopped dill or fennel leaves*
> *1 teaspoon light miso*

Indian

> *1 onion, finely chopped*
> *2 tablespoons sunflower oil*

Sauté until soft. Then add

> *1 teaspoon turmeric*
> *½ teaspoon ground coriander*
> *½ teaspoon ground cumin*

and cook for a few minutes more.
> *Remove from the heat. Add*

> *juice of 1 lemon*

Cool and stir into the mayonnaise.

Hot Vegetable Dishes

Arabian Stuffed Aubergines (Eggplant)

Serves 4
Oven: 180°C/350°F/gas 4

---

2 medium aubergines (eggplant),
    good and firm
enough water to cover

Drop the whole aubergines into a large pan of boiling water, boil gently for 15 minutes. Drain and cool. Cut in half lengthways (if you can keep half the stalk on each, it looks nice). Carefully cut the flesh into pieces, keeping the skin whole.

---

4 tablespoons olive oil
4 cloves
2 bay leaves
1 cinammon stick
1 medium onion, finely chopped
4 garlic cloves, finely sliced
2 tablespoons tomato purée
    (tomato paste)
2 tomatoes, finely chopped
75 g (3 oz/½ cup) pine nuts
75 g (3 oz/½ cup) currants
½ teaspoon ground black
    pepper
2 tablespoons tamari

Heat the oil in a heavy based pan with the cloves, bay leaves and cinammon. Add the onion and garlic, soften for a few minutes. Add the tomato purée (tomato paste) and cook a minute or two longer before adding the rest of the ingredients, along with the chopped flesh of the aubergine. Cook and stir for 5 minutes.

---

25 g (1 oz/½ cup) chopped fresh
    basil or coriander (cilantro)
2 tablespoons olive oil

Stir in the fresh herbs and pile into the aubergine (eggplant) skins. Place in a greased ovenproof dish. Drizzle with a little olive oil and bake for 20–30 minutes.

Serve with rice and salad.

Malay-spiced Tofu

Serves 4–6
Oven: 220°C/425°F/gas 7

---

100 g (4 oz/⅓ cup) peeled and
   grated fresh root ginger
15 garlic cloves, peeled
2 fresh or dried red chillies
juice of 1 large lemon

Blend to a paste in a blender or with a pestle
and mortar.

---

500 g (1 lb 2 oz/2 cups) fresh
   organic tofu, cut into bite-sized
   pieces
120 ml (4 fl oz/½ cup) tamari
4 tablespoons cornflour
   (cornstarch) or arrowroot

Mix gently with half the ginger paste, and leave
to marinate (overnight if you can, but allow about
30 minutes if you've made a spontaneous decision
to cook this dish).

---

4 tablespoons cold-pressed oil
4 onions, chopped
6 star anise

Get the oil very hot and fry the onions and star anise
together until the onions are good and brown.
Stir in the remaining ginger paste and gently add the
tofu. Keep the heat high and stir and scrape the pan
gently and continually (a non-stick pan – without a
plastic or wooden handle, of course – helps if you
have one big enough; a heavy enamelled iron one is
also good). Place in the oven for 20–25 minutes,
scraping and turning gently once during cooking time.
Serve with rice or noodles.

Stir-fry of Asparagus and Brazil Nuts

Serves 4–6

---

1 tablespoon arrowroot or cornflour
  (cornstarch)
2 tablespoons water
1 tablespoon tamari
1 tablespoon miso
150 ml (¼ pint/½ cup) water

Mix the arrowroot or cornflour (cornstarch) with
the water until smooth, then blend with the other
ingredients to form a smooth paste.

---

2 tablespoons sunflower oil
1 leek or onion, thinly sliced
1 tablespoon grated fresh root
  ginger
3 garlic cloves, grated
450 g (1 lb/3 cups) fresh asparagus
  spears, sliced diagonally into
  2.5-cm (1-in) lengths
100 g (4 oz/1 cup) Brazil nuts,
  sliced
2 teaspoons toasted sesame seeds

Heat the oil in a wok over quite a high heat. Toss
in the leek or onion, ginger, and garlic. Stir and
cook for 2 minutes, then add the asparagus and nuts.
Stir and cook for 5 more minutes.
Pour in the miso mixture. Stir, reduce the heat and
cook until the asparagus is just tender.
Sprinkle with the sesame seeds.

 Serve with rice or buckwheat noodles.

Aromatic Glazed Turnips

Serves 4–6
Oven: 190°C/375°F/gas 5

2 tablespoons honey 2 tablespoons olive oil 3 bay leaves sprig of fresh thyme (optional)	Melt together in a roasting pan.

16 baby turnips (approximately), trimmed and scrubbed 8 whole shallots or 4 small onions cut into quarters 120 ml (4 fl oz/½ cup) water	Add to the pan. Stir to coat the vegetables and bake for about 35 minutes, until the turnips are tender and well browned. Turn out onto a warmed serving dish and scrape and stir the pan juices then pour them over the top of the turnips to serve.

Creamed Garlic Potatoes

Serves 4–6
Oven: 220°C/425°F/gas 7

6 or 8 medium potatoes, peeled and chopped 6 garlic cloves 300 ml (½ pint/1¼ cups) soya milk water to cover	Boil together until the potatoes are tender and drain. (You can keep the cooking liquid for making a soup.)

4 tablespoons olive oil grating of nutmeg pinch of ground black pepper	Add to the cooked potatoes and mash really well. (If you have a mouli you will be able to achieve the ultimate in smoothness.) Serve as it is or you can pop it in a greased dish and brown in the oven for 10 minutes.

Braised Sweet and Sour Carrots

Serves 4–6

---

3 tablespoons sunflower oil *6 medium carrots, scrubbed and* *cut into long pieces*	Saute together over a high heat until the carrots are just, but only just, browning.

---

100 g (4 oz/½ cup) honey	Add to the pan, stir and sizzle well for 4–5 minutes. Reduce the heat, cover and cook very gently for 5 minutes.

---

150 ml (¼ pint/½ cup) cider *vinegar* *4 tablespoons tamari*	Remove the lid, increase the heat and stir in vinegar and tamari. Simmer until the carrots are soft.

---

2 tablespoons arrowroot or
   cornflour (cornstarch) or potato
   flour, mixed to a smooth runny
   paste with
150 ml (¼ pint/½cup) apple
   juice
	Add to the pan and stir well, until thickened and clear.
	Check for flavour balance. It may need a spoonful more of honey or vinegar depending on your taste.

 Serve with a stir-fry of vegetables and buckwheat noodles, or try it with Malay-spiced Tofu and Rice.

Cauliflower, Tofu and Nut Bake

Serves 4–6
Oven: 220°C/425°F/gas 7

---

1 large cauliflower, cut into very
*   small pieces and cooked until*
*   just tender*
225 g (8 oz/1 cup) fresh tofu,
*   chopped*
2 tablespoons tamari
1 teaspoon ground black pepper
1 teaspoon ground nutmeg

Place just half the cooked cauliflower and half the tofu pieces in a food processor with the tamari and spices. Whizz to just blend, but do not make the mixture too smooth. Mashing it well works too. Gently stir in the remaining pieces of cauliflower and tofu.

---

50 g (2 oz/½ cup) walnuts
50 g (2 oz/½ cup) sunflower seeds

Roast them for 8 minutes on a baking sheet in the oven.
Turn the oven down to 190°C/375°F/gas 5.

---

100 g (4 oz /2 cups) soft wholemeal
*   (wholewheat) breadcrumbs*
handful of fresh parsley, chopped
300 ml (½ pint/1 cup) soya milk
2 teaspoons tamari

Gently fold all the ingredients, except the tamari, together with the cauliflower mixture and nuts and seeds, making sure your creamy cauliflower mixture is evenly spread through the breadcrumbs. You may find this easier to do if you soak the breadcrumbs in the soya milk before you start mixing. However you do it, be gentle and then spoon the whole lot into an oiled ovenproof dish, splash the top with the tamari and bake for 25 minutes.

Chinese-style
Stir-fried Vegetables

Serves 4–6

---

3 tablespoons sunflower oil

1 large onion, sliced vertically

1 teaspoon roasted sesame oil

3 garlic cloves, finely grated

15 g (½ oz) fresh ginger root,
    peeled and finely grated

3 star anise (optional)

Heat the oil in a large wok. Toss in the onions
and other ingredients and cook until just softened.
Keep them on the move while you add your choice
of the following selection – 3 or 4 work best. (Those
at the top of the list need the longest cooking time
so put them in first and stir a minute or two before
adding your other choices.)

---

2 carrots, very thinly sliced
    diagonally

1 head of broccoli, very thinly
    sliced

2 celery sticks, thinly sliced
    diagonally

1 green or red pepper
    (bell pepper, thinly sliced)

4 medium mushrooms, sliced

10 button mushrooms, halved

175 g (6 oz/2 cups) mixed wild
    mushrooms

25 g (1 oz/¼ cup) dry arame
    or hijiki seaweed (soaked for
    10 minutes in hot water)

100 g (4 oz/2 cups) shredded
    cabbage

100 g (4 oz/2 cups) shredded
    Chinese greens

100 g (4 oz/2 cups) mung
    beansprouts

Toss around in the wok over quite a fierce heat
until everything is heated through.

---

3 tablespoons tamari

Pour over the mixture.

Sprinkle with sesame seeds and serve with rice.

Courgette (Zucchini) and Potato Rosti

Serves 4–6

---

3 medium potatoes, skins left on,
  coarsely grated
1 courgette (zucchini), grated
1 teaspoon ground black pepper
1 teaspoon black poppy seeds
pinch of fresh thyme leaves
1 tablespoon rice flour

Mix together well, then leave for 10 minutes before squeezing the liquid out firmly (twisting the mixture in a clean teatowel (dishcloth) is quite effective).

---

3 tablespoons olive oil
1 teaspoon tamari

Heat the oil in a heavy frying pan (a non-stick one helps). Put the potato mixture in the pan and press gently to an even thickness. Cook gently without stirring or covering for 20 minutes.
Turn the rosti over. This is considerably easier if you have another oiled pan to place over the top and invert the whole thing carefully into this other pan. If not, use an oiled plate and slide the turned rosti back into the same pan. Cook gently for 15–20 minutes more. Sprinkle with the tamari, slice and serve hot.

Creamed Fennel

Serves 4–6

---

1 large onion, roughly chopped
2 teaspoons whole fennel seeds
2 tablespoons olive oil

Sauté together until softened.

---

1 small potato, peeled and chopped
2 fresh fennel bulbs, finely
    chopped, including any nice
    feathery bits on the top
½ teaspoon ground black
    pepper
½ teaspoon ground nutmeg

Add to the pan and stir well. Cover and cook over a
low heat for 8–10 minutes.

---

300 ml (½ pint/1 cup) vegetable
    stock or water with 1 tablespoon
    low-salt stock (bouillon) powder
ground black pepper
grating of nutmeg

Add to the pan and keep simmering gently for about
20–25 minutes, until the fennel is very tender and
almost all of the liquid has evaporated. Leave to cool
a little, then purée in a blender or food processor.
Sprinkle with a little pepper and a grating or two of
nutmeg and serve hot.

---

*This is lovely served with a nut roast or vegetable pie,
but if instead of blending it, you chop about 500g
(8 oz/2 cups) fresh tofu over it and then pop it under a
hot grill (broiler) for 5 minutes, you have a delicious
lunch or light supper.*

Creamy Golden Casserole

Serves 4–6
Oven: 190°C/375°F/gas 5

---

225 g (8 oz/1 cup) yellow split peas
600 ml (1 pint/2 cups) water or
   vegetable stock
1 teaspoon low-salt stock (bouillon)
   powder

Cook gently together for 30–35 minutes until soft.
Check the pan from time to time to ensure that they
do not dry out before they are cooked.

---

1 kg (2¼ lbs/6 cups) yellow
  - or orange-fleshed squash,
  deseeded and thickly sliced
2 tablespoons tamari
50 g (2 oz/½ cup) creamed coconut
  or fresh, grated coconut or
  dessicated (shredded) coconut
  soaked in 250 ml (½ pint/1 cup)
  boiling water

Mix with the split peas in a large casserole dish.

---

2 tablespoons olive or sunflower oil
2 teaspoons black mustard seeds
bay leaf
1 onion, sliced
1 teaspoon turmeric

Heat the oil in a small, heavy based pan.
Add the mustard seeds and stir at arm's length
until they stop popping.
Add the bay leaf and onion and soften for
10 minutes.Stir in the turmeric, cook a for a few more
minutes and tip onto squash mixture. Give it one stir,
cover and bake for approximately 35–40 minutes,
until the squash is soft.

Serve with rice or scoop up with pitta bread or chapatis.

Creamy Leek and Mushroom Croustade

Serves 4–6
Oven: 250°C/450°F/gas 8

25 g (1 oz) soya margarine
2 tablespoons olive oil
100 g (4 oz/2 cups) soft brown
  breadcrumbs
100 g (4 oz/²/₃ cup) ground
  hazelnuts
50 g (2 oz/²/₃ cup) finely chopped
  almonds
1 teaspoon tarragon
2 garlic cloves, crushed

Melt the margarine and oil together and mix thoroughly with the other ingredients. Press into a greased ovenproof cake tin or flan dish. Use the back of a spoon to press it down firmly. Bake for 15 minutes.

2 leeks, finely chopped
100 g (4 oz/1 cup) sliced
  mushrooms
2 tablespoons olive oil
1 teaspoon ground black
  pepper
1 teaspoon ground nutmeg
50 g (2 oz/¹/₂ cup) wholemeal
  (wholwheat) or rice flour
300 ml (¹/₂ pint/1 cup) soya milk
1 tablespoon olive oil
1 tablespoon tamari

Sauté the leeks and mushrooms in the oil with the pepper and nutmeg. Cover and cook over a low heat for 10 minutes. Stir in the flour and slowly add the milk, stirring all the time. Simmer gently to thicken. Spoon the mixture onto the croustade base. Splash the top with a little olive oil and tamari and return to the oven for about 10 minutes.

Lovely with Creamed Garlic Potatoes and broccoli or a green salad.

Galette of Parsnips and Cashew Nuts

Serves 4–6
Oven: 190°C/375°F/Gas 5

1.5 kg (3 lbs) parsnips, scrubbed
   and chopped into 1-cm (½-in)
   slices

Cook in boiling water for 10 minutes.

---

2 onions, finely chopped
3 tablespoons olive oil
2 teaspoons dried sage
2 teaspoons dried thyme

Soften the onions in a pan with the oil
and add the herbs.

---

450 g (1 lb/3 cups) whole cashew
   nuts
2 tablespoons tamari
1 teaspoon black pepper
100 g (4 oz/2 cups) soft brown
   breadcrumbs
50 g (2 oz/1 cup) chopped fresh
   parsley

Finely chop half the cashews and mix well with everything but the parsnips and parsley. Grease 20–25-cm (8–10-in) loose-bottomed cake tin or ovenproof dish, spread a layer of whole cashew nuts over the base, then a layer of parsnip slices. It looks good if you stand some round the side too. Spread the breadcrumb mixture over the top and a thick sprinkling of fresh parsley over that. Continue layering the ingredients, ending with parsnips. Cover with foil and bake for 35–40 minutes. Remove from oven, let stand for 10 minutes, then turn out onto a warm plate. Slice with a sharp knife and serve with gravy or the Bright Red Pepper (Bell Pepper) Sauce (see page 25).

Fresh tarragon makes a good alternative to the parsley and the creamed garlic sauce is good with it too.

Ginger and Sesame Carrots

Serves 4–6

---

3 tablespoons olive or sunflower oil
25 g (1 oz/¼ cup) sesame seeds
25 g (1 oz/¼ cup) fresh root ginger,
    peeled and grated
2 garlic cloves, grated (optional)
6 medium carrots, scrubbed and
    cut into matchsticks or thin
    diagonal slices

Heat the oil and sesame seeds together in a wok or an enamelled iron casserole. When the seeds begin to pop, stand back and add the ginger, garlic, if using, and stir. Add the carrots and stir well. Lower the heat a little, cover and cook for 6–10 minutes, stirring once during this time.

Fresh parsley or coriander (cilantro) is delicious stirred in just before serving. Finely shredded raw spinach or chard leaves also go well with this and should also be added at the last minute. As a quick snack, this is scrumptious stuffed into warm, brown pitta bread with a drizzle of light tahini and tamari.

Grilled (Broiled) Aubergines (Eggplant) with Salsa Verde

Serves 4–6

---

*2 medium aubergines (eggplant),
   cut lengthways into 5-mm
   (¼-in) slices*
4 tablespoons olive oil

Brush the slices with a little oil and grill (broil)
on both sides until golden brown and soft
(8–10 minutes).

---

*2 garlic cloves, peeled and roughly
   chopped*
2 tablespoons parlsey
2 tablespoons fresh basil
2 tablespoons pine nuts or almonds
*½ teaspoon ground black
   pepper*
*100 ml (3½ fl oz/scant ½ cup)
   olive oil*

Place in a blender and process to a smoothish paste.

---

2 large tomatoes, finely chopped

Layer the aubergine (eggplant) slices alternately
with the tomatoes. Pour over the salsa.

---

*Nice just warm or chilled served with hot bread, rice
or couscous.*

Parsnips and Carrots with Sesame and Maple Glaze

Serves 4–6
Oven: 190°C/375°F/gas 5

2 good-sized parsnips, scrubbed
and cubed
4 carrots, scrubbed and cubed

Toss the carrots into a pan of boiling water.
Return to the boil and cook for 5 minutes.
Add the parsnips and boil for a further
5 minutes. Drain.

2 tablespoons sesame seeds
2 tablespoons olive oil
2 tablespoons maple syrup
1 teaspoon tamari (optional)
zest (grated rind) and juice of ½ an
orange

Stir gently into the carrots and parsnips. Turn into
a roasting tin and bake in the oven for
20–25 minutes, until just browning.

Works well with parboiled new potatoes too.

Parsnip Dabs

Makes approximately 12–14
Oven: 190°C/375°F/gas 5

750 g (1½ lbs/4 cups) parsnips, scrubbed and diced (peel them if they seem a bit tough or elderly)	Boil in water until soft (approximately 15 minutes). Drain and mash – don't worry if there are a few lumps.
1 tablespoon olive oil *2 teaspoons dried or fresh tarragon* *1 medium onion, finely chopped*	Fry gently in the oil until the onion is very soft.
500g (2oz/½ cup) finely chopped walnuts *1 tablespoon tamari* *1 teaspoon ground black pepper* *2 tablespoons soya flour or rice flour*	Mix well into the parsnips and onions. Allow to cool.
225g (8oz/ 2 cups) soft brown breadcrumbs	Divide the parsnip mixture into 12 and form into balls (wetting your hands helps with this process). Roll the balls around, one by one, in the breadcrumbs and gently press onto an oiled baking sheet. If you have any crumbs left over, pat them onto the tops of the 'dabs'. Bake for 20 minutes.
	A really green vegetable is the natural partner to these, such as broccoli or curly kale. Try Bright Red Pepper (Bell Pepper) Sauce (see page 25) or apple sauce with them too.

Potato and Mushroom Curry

Serves 4–6

---

4 tablespoons sunflower oil
1 cinnamon stick
4 whole cloves
2 bay leaves
2 teaspoons cumin seeds

Fry together for 2–3 minutes.

---

2 medium onions, finely chopped
2 x 5-cm (2-in) chunks of fresh root
   ginger, peeled and finely grated
4 garlic cloves, finely grated
1 teaspoon tomato purée
   (tomato paste)
4 tomatoes, chopped

Add to the oil and fry for a few minutes, stirring
all the time.
Reduce the heat, cover and cook for a further
10 minutes.

---

2 teaspoons turmeric
2 teaspoons ground cumin
2 teaspoons ground coriander

Add to the onions, stir well and fry for
2–3 minutes longer.

---

4 medium potatoes, cut into
   approximately 2.5-cm (1-in)
   cubes
350 g (12 oz/3 cups) whole button
   mushrooms

Stir into the pan, making sure that the
potatoes are well coated with the spices.

---

300 ml (½ pint/1 cup) water
2 tablespoons tamari

Add to the pan. Stir well, cover and cook over a
very low heat for 30 minutes. Stir after 15 minutes
and add a little more water if it is beginning to stick.
Cook gently until the potatoes are really soft.
Serve with rice and a wedge of lemon or raita.

Starry Quinoa Pilaff – Persian Style

Serves 4–6

---

900 ml (1½ pints/3¾ cups) water
350 g (12 oz/2 cups) quinoa

Bring the water (twice the amount of grain you have) to the boil. Add the quinoa, return to the boil, cover and simmer very gently for 15 minutes. Tip into a colander.

---

150 ml (¼ pint/½ cup) olive oil
450 g (1 lb/2½ cups) small, firm
    okra
    (ladies fingers), sliced quite
    thinly to form little stars
2 tablespoons tomato purée
    (tomato paste)
225 g (8 oz/1 cup) peas
1 medium onion, very finely
    chopped
3 garlic cloves, thinly sliced
2 tomatoes, finely chopped
2 teaspoons cumin seeds
1 teaspoon ground black
    pepper

Heat the oil in a large pan (a wok is ideal for this) over a high heat. Add the okra slices and toss about quickly until just browning. Lower the heat a little, mix in the tomato purée (tomato paste) and fry for a minute or two. Add the other ingredients and keep stirring and tossing together for 5 minutes or so. Lower the heat, cover and cook for 8 minutes more. Uncover, reduce any liquid that is left over a high heat for a couple of minutes and add the quinoa. Mix well. Cover and let stand for 10 minutes.

---

50 g (2 oz/1 cup) chopped fresh
    coriander (cilantro)
2 tablespoons tamari (optional)

Toss into the pilaff as you serve.

Braised Squash
with Green Lentils

Serves 4–6

---

*120 g (4½ oz/½ cup) whole green
   lentils*

Cook them in water or vegetable stock for
40–45 minutes, until soft.

---

2 tablespoons olive oil
*10 spring onions (scallions),
   chopped into 2.5-cm (1-in)
   lengths*
2 garlic cloves, peeled and sliced
sprig of fresh thyme
2 bay leaves
1 teaspoon ground black pepper
*750 g (1½ lbs/5 cups)
   yellow-fleshed sweet squash
   (butternut, red onion or sweet
   pumpkin, etc.) cut into bite-size
   pieces, seeds and fibres removed
   (if young and fresh, you
   shouldn't need to peel it)*

Heat the oil, soften the onions and garlic with the
herbs and seasoning.
Add the squash. Stir, mix together
and cook gently for 6–7 minutes. Add the cooked
lentils and stir in gently.

---

*450 g (1 lb/2 cups) fresh tomatoes,
   finely chopped or 400-g (14-oz)
   can tomatoes, finely chopped
   with juice*
1 tablespoon tamari
juice of 1 lemon

Add to the pan and cook very gently for another
20 minutes or so, stirring occasionally. The dish
should be soft and moist, but not runny, so allow
some of the liquid to evaporate.

Provençal Vegetables

Serves 4–6

---

3 tablespoons olive oil
1 large onion
2 garlic cloves
1 teaspoon dried oregano
1 teaspoon dried thyme

Soften together in a large, heavy based pan with a lid.

---

4 tablespoons tomato purée
  (tomato paste)
4 ripe tomatoes, chopped
1 aubergine (eggplant), chopped
3 medium courgettes (zucchini),
  chopped
1 green or red pepper (bell pepper),
  chopped
1 teaspoon ground black pepper
1 tablespoon tamari

Fry the tomato purée (tomato paste) with the onion mixture for a few minutes, until the oil begins to separate, stirring over a medium heat. Add the other ingredients. When the mixture is sizzling and well mixed, reduce the heat, cover and simmer very gently for 35–40 minutes, either on the stove or in the oven (180°C/350°F/gas 4). Uncover and cook for a further 5 minutes to reduce a little of the liquid, stirring as necessary.

Soubise Tartlets

Serves 6
Oven: as specified
throughout the recipe

---

175 g (6 oz/ generous 1 cup)
    wholemeal (wholewheat) flour
    with bran sifted out
50 g (2 oz/¹⁄₃ cup) unbleached
    organic white flour
50 g (2 oz/¹⁄₃ cup) soya margarine
4 tablespoons olive oil
50 ml (2 fl oz/¹⁄₄ cup) ground
    sesame seeds
cold water, to bind

Make a shortcrust pastry (see page 115) using enough cold water to bind the dough together (how much you will need will vary depending on the absorbancy of the flour). Roll out quite thinly and use to line six 10 cm (4 in) tartlet cases. Bake blind for 15 minutes in a preheated 190°C/375°F/gas 5 oven.

---

3 medium onions, thinly sliced
3 tablespoons olive oil
1 teaspoon fresh or dried rosemary
¹⁄₂ teaspoon grated nutmeg
1 teaspoon ground black pepper
1 teaspoon low-salt stock (bouillon)
    powder

Sauté gently together until the onions soften. Turn down to a very low heat, cover and cook for 15 minutes. Stir once or twice during this time. The onions should then be soft and juicy. Cool a little.

---

100 g (4 oz/¹⁄₂ cup) fresh organic
    tofu
generous half of the onion
    mixture
grated nutmeg, to taste
sprig of rosemary, to garnish

Blend in a food processor or blender. Spread some of the cooked onion mixture in the base of each pastry case. Spoon tofu cream over the onion mixture and sprinkle grated nutmeg over the top, then bake for 15–20 minutes in a 180°C/350°F/gas 4 oven until the filling is just set. Garnish with the pieces of the rosemary sprig.

Spicy Oven Fries

Serves 4–6
Oven: 200°C/375°F/Gas 6

---

2 tablespoons olive oil
1 tablespoon tomato purée
(tomato paste)
1 teaspoon paprika
1 tablespoon tamari
1 teaspoon ground black pepper

Whisk together in a large mixing bowl.

---

3 or 4 large potatoes, scrubbed and
cut into fairly fat 'fingers'
(approximately 12–14 from
each potato)

Toss the potato fingers in the mixture, making sure
they are evenly covered.
Turn into a roasting tin and bake for 35–40 minutes,
until soft in the middle and a bit crunchy around
the edges.

---

*Try serving these with a creamy soup for a delicious
change to the usual soup accompaniments.*

Spring Vegetables

Serves 4–6

---

*225 g (8 oz/1 cup) dried flageolet
  or cannellini beans*
15 baby carrots, scrubbed
10 tiny onions or shallots
1 cauliflower, divided into florets
*2 little gem lettuces or firm lettuce
  hearts, quartered*
*100 g (4 oz/1 cup) chopped fresh
  mint*
*2 tablespoons low-salt stock
  (bouillon) powder*
1 teaspoon ground black pepper
*450 g (1 lb/2 cups) tiny scrubbed
  new potatoes*
1.25 litres (2¼ pints/5 cups) water
10 garlic cloves, peeled

Cook the dried beans until tender, drain and return to the cleaned pan together with all the other ingredients. Bring to the boil and simmer gently until the potatoes are tender, about 35 minutes.

---

*450 g (1 lb/2 cups) fresh peas or
  mangetout (snow peas)*

Add to the pan and cook for 5 minutes more.

Serve with a sprinkling of fresh mint. This dish needs nothing else but a spoon!

Turkish Green Beans

Serves 4–6

---

2 tablespoons olive oil
2 bay leaves
4 cloves
1 cinnamon stick
2 large garlic cloves, sliced

Heat the oil, add the bay leaves, spices and garlic and stir for half a minute.

---

1 onion, finely chopped
3 large tomatoes, finely chopped
450 g (1 lb/4 cups) green beans
1 teaspoon ground black
   pepper
150 ml (¼ pint/½ cup) water

Toss into the spiced oil, sizzle gently and stir over a high heat for 3–4 minutes. Add the water, reduce the heat, cover tightly and cook gently for approximately 20–25 minutes, until the beans are soft.

---

3 teaspoons cider vinegar
1 teaspoon ground cinnamon
1 teaspoon ground nutmeg

Stir into the beans. Sizzle for 3–4 minutes more and serve hot, warm or cold.

Vegetable and Herb Quiche

Serves 4–6
Oven: 180°C/350°F/gas 4

---

1 cooked 23–25-cm (8–10-in) wholemeal (wholewheat) pastry case
275g (10 oz/2 cups) cooked vegetables of your choice, diced

Scatter the vegetables over the base of the pastry case.

275–350 g (10–12 oz/2 cups) fresh tofu
25 g (1 oz/1 cup) chopped fresh herbs
2 tablespoons olive oil
2 tablespoons tamari
150 ml (¼ pint/½ cup) soya milk
1 teaspoon ground black pepper
1 teaspoon light tahini (optional)

Whizz together in a blender or food processor and pour over the vegetables. Tap gently a couple of times onto the work surface to settle the cream around the vegetables. Pop into the oven and bake for 30 minutes, until the filling is just set and browning a little.

Here are some ideas for vegetable and herb combinations:

- *potatoes, leeks, chives, parsley, nutmeg*
- *courgettes (zucchini), mushrooms, tarragon, parsley, chervil*
- *tomatoes, onions, courgettes (zucchini), garlic, oregano, marjoram*
- *squash, onion, thyme, garlic*
- *cooked beans, onions, leeks, sage, thyme.*

Aromatic White Beans

Serves 4–6

---

225 g (8 oz/2 cups) dried white
    beans (cannellini or butter
    (lima) beans)

Soak the beans overnight.
Next day, cook them in water for about 2 hours,
or until soft.

---

2 tablespoons sunflower oil
1 green pepper (bell pepper), finely
    chopped
5-cm (2-in) piece of fresh root
    ginger, peeled and finely grated
3 garlic cloves, peeled and finely
    grated
1 medium onion, finely chopped
1 teaspoon cumin seeds
1 teaspoon ground coriander
½ teaspoon chilli powder or
    paprika (optional)

Fry and stir gently together until soft.

---

4 fresh tomatoes, finely chopped
1 teaspoon tomato purée (tomato
    paste)
ground black pepper
tamari or lemon juice, to garnish
good handful of chopped coriander
    (cilantro) leaves

Add all but the black pepper, tamari or lemon juice
and coriander (cilantro) to the spicy vegetables,
stir well, increase the heat a little, then add the
beans. Stir well and cook for a further 4–5 minutes.
Reduce the heat and cook for a further
10–15 minutes.
Season with a little black pepper and tamari or
lemon juice and sprinkle with the fresh coriander
(cilantro) before serving. Good hot or cold.

---

*If you have any left over, it also makes a great sandwich
spread if you whizz it in a blender. Then you can pile it
on pitta bread or hot wholemeal (wholewheat) toast.*

Braised Butter Beans and Lettuce

Serves 4–6

---

4 tablespoons olive oil
12 whole shallots or 2 onions,
    finely chopped
4 whole garlic cloves
450 g (1 lb/2 cups) cooked butter
    (lima) beans i.e. 1 cup dried
    (see page 13 for cooking time)
1 large, long-leaved lettuce
    (e.g. Cos), shredded
1 teaspoon dried or fresh thyme
handful of fresh parsley, chopped
1 teaspoon ground black pepper
5 tablespoons water
1 tablespoon cider vinegar
2 small strips orange rind (zest)

Heat the oil in a heavy casserole.
Roll the shallots or onions and garlic around in
the oil for a couple of minutes.
Lower the heat a little and add all the other
ingredients. Stir well. Cover and cook slowly for
approximately 30 minutes.

Lovely with rice.

Couscous Pilaff

Serves 4–6
Oven: 180°C/350°F/gas 4

---

350 g (12 oz/2 cups) couscous
1.2 litres (2 pints/4 cups) hot water

Soak the couscous in the hot water for 30 minutes.

---

3 tablespoons olive oil
4 teaspoons cumin seeds
1 cinnamon stick

Heat the oil in a deep roasting dish or casserole and toast the seeds and cinnamon in it a little bit.

---

1 onion, finely chopped
450 g (1 lb/8 cups) finely shredded
  beetroot (beet) leaves and stems
  or spinach or Swiss chard (silver
  beet)
100 g (4 oz/1 cup) currants
1 tablespoon low-salt stock
  (bouillon) powder
1 teaspoon ground black pepper
grated zest (rind) and juice of
  1 lemon
handful of green herbs (e.g. parsley,
  oregano, basil, coriander
  (cilantro)

Toss the onion and beetroot (beet) or chard (silver beet) into the roasting dish or casserole and stir until they have given up their juices and the liquid has reduced well.
Tip in the soaked couscous and the other ingredients, except the herbs. Don't worry if there is a little water still unabsorbed, but, if it looks like more than a cupful, drain it off before adding the couscous to the pan. Stir well, cover tightly and cook for 10–15 minutes. Sprinkle with the herbs and serve.

A good variation is to stir in some grated, raw carrot or courgette (zucchini) or fresh peas with the juice of a lemon before serving.

Mung Bean and Sage Cottage Pie

Serves 4–6
Oven: 220°C/425°F/gas 7

---

50 g (1 lb/2 cups) mung beans
   or aduki beans
6 garlic cloves

Cook the beans for 45 minutes in boiling water to which the garlic cloves have been added. Reserve the water for later use in this recipe if desired.

1.5 kg (3 lbs) potatoes, scrubbed
300 ml (½ pint/1 cup) soya milk
1 tablespoon olive oil

Boil potatoes with their skins on until they are tender. Then drain and mashed well, adding the milk and oil.

---

50 g (2 oz/½ cup) cornflour
   (cornstarch) 300 ml (½ pint/
   1 cup) apple juice
600 ml (1 pint/2 cups) water or
   cooking liquid from mung beans
150 ml (¼ pint/½ cup) tamari
1 teaspoon low-salt stock (bouillon)
   powder or yeast spread
   (Vitam R or Vecon)

Mix the cornflour (cornstarch) to a smooth paste with a little of the liquid, then carefully mix in the rest of the ingredients.

---

2 onions, finely chopped
3 tablespoons fresh or dried sage
   leaves
4 tablespoons olive oil
2 carrots, grated
1 teaspoon ground black pepper

Saute together gently until soft, about 10–15 minutes. Add the mung beans, stir well and pour in the apple juice mixture and simmer, stirring until thickened. Tip into a greased ovenproof dish, top with the mashed potato and bake for about 20 minutes, until just browned.

Moroccan-style Braised Vegetables and Butter Beans

Serves 4–6
Oven: 180°C/350°F/gas 4

---

4 tablespoons olive oil
2 teaspoons fennel seeds
1 or 2 cinnamon sticks
3 teaspoons dried oregano

Heat the oil gently with the seeds, spice and herb in a deep roasting tin or casserole.

---

4 garlic cloves, sliced
3 onions, cut into fat wedges
1 teaspoon ground cloves or
   6 whole cloves
2 teaspoons ground cinnamon
1 teaspoon ground nutmeg
2 teaspoons low-salt stock
   (bouillon) powder
1 teaspoon ground black pepper

Soften onions and garlic a little in herby oil, then add spices and bouillon powder. Cook and stir a few more minutes.

---

450 g (1 lb/3 cups) butternut or
   sweet orange-fleshed squash or
   sweet potato, cut into 2.5-m
   (1-in) slices or chunky dice
450 g (1 lb/3 cups) carrots, scrubbed
   and cut lengthways into 4
2 bulbs (heads) fennel, trimmed and
   cut into wedges from root to tip
450 g (1 lb/2 cups) cooked butter
   (lima) beans or chickpeas
   (garbanzos) or kidney or
   flageolet beans 1 cup dried
   (see page 000 for cooking time)

Toss into the spicy mixture over a gentle heat. Mix very well.

---

4 ripe tomatoes, chopped or
   blended to a pulp or 1 can
   tomatoes, whizzed in a blender

Stir into the vegetables, cover and bake in the oven for 35–40 minutes, or until the carrots are soft.

---

4 tablespoons cider vinegar
handful fresh chopped chives
   (optional)

Sprinkle the vinegar over as soon as you take the dish from the oven, cover, leave for 3 minutes. Serve sprinkled with the fresh chopped chives.

Poppy Seed and Sour Cream Pasta

Serves 4–6
Oven: 180°C/350°F/gas 4

---

225 g (8 oz/2½ cups)
   wholemeal (wholewheat) pasta

Cook until tender. Drain.

---

85 ml (3 fl oz/scant ½ cup) lemon
   juice
2 tablespoons olive oil
1 tablespoon miso
1 tablespoon tamari
225 g (8 oz/1 cup) tofu
15 g (½ oz/1/3 cup) chopped fresh
   chives

Blend until smooth in a food processor (if you use a blender, you may need to add a little water to keep it moving).

---

25 g (1 oz/¼ cup) poppy seeds
ground black pepper, to taste
pinch of paprika

Stir the poppy seeds into the cream and mix into the pasta.
Turn into a greased, ovenproof dish, sprinkle with some ground black pepper and paprika and bake for about 20 minutes.

Delicious with baked or steamed courgettes (zucchini) sprinkled with a little tarragon.

The 'Good for any Vegetable' Stuffing

Makes sufficient to stuff quantities of vegetables given below
Oven: Follow the settings given in the recipe

---

2 tablespoons olive oil
2 small onions, finely chopped
2 celery sticks, finely chopped
1 carrot, grated
1 teaspoon dried basil
1 teaspoon dried oregano
½ teaspoon thyme
½ teaspoon sage
1 teaspoon ground cumin
2 teaspoons tomato purée (tomato paste)

Sauté together very gently in a heavy based pan. Stir well for 2–3 minutes, then reduce the heat, cover and cook for a further 5 minutes.

---

300 ml (½ pint/1 cup) vegetable stock or water
1 tablespoon tamari
350 g (12 oz/2 cups) cooked rice or millet or buckwheat or grain of your choice or 1 cup raw (see page 000 for cooking time) or 225 g (8 oz/3 cups) soft breadcrumbs
4 tablespoons olive oil

Add to the vegetable mixture. Stir really well, remove the pan from the heat, cover and let stand for 5 minutes before using to stuff any vegetables that you have hollowed out or have conveniently got a space in them! The cooking time will vary depending on the vegetables, but see below for guidelines. Drizzle or brush with olive oil before baking.

---

12 whole tomatoes – 20 minutes at 190°C/375°F/gas 5

6 large peppers (bell peppers), halved – 30 minutes at 180°C/350°F/gas 4

10 large courgettes (zucchini) – 35–45 minutes (covered for first 30 minutes) at 180°C/350°F/gas 4

2 large-medium squash, halved – approximately 20 minutes per 500g (1lb) at 180°C/350°F/gas 4

8 whole small squash – 40 minutes at 190°C/375°F/gas 5

Lovely with rice.

Desserts and Sweet Creams

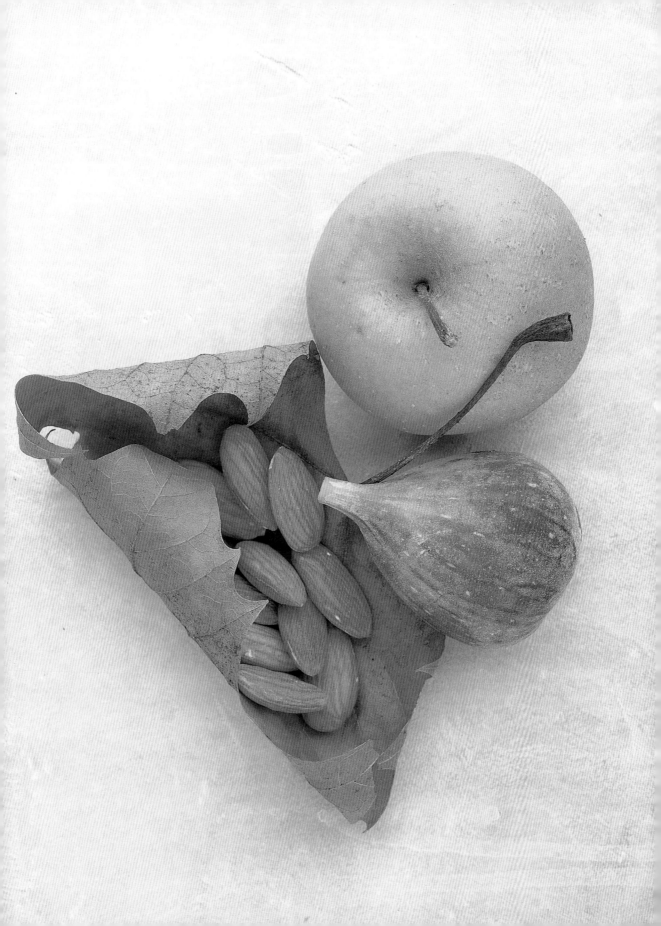

Poached Pears with Fresh Strawberry Coulis

Serves 4

---

4 firm, ripe pears, peeled, cored and halved
300 ml (½ pint/1 cup) apple juice concentrate or natural fruit concentrate (strawberry or exotic fruit is very good)
600 ml (1 pint/2 cups) water

Place the pears flat side down in a deep roasting dish or casserole. Add the liquids, cover and cook gently until the pears are soft – approximately 40 minutes. (Keep the heat low – they don't like to boil madly.) Remove the pears to a serving dish. Boil the juices left in the pan to reduce to about half the volume to form a syrup, and pour over the pears. Chill.

---

450 g (1 lb/3 cups) fresh strawberries
juice of 1 lemon
2 tablespoons syrup from the pears

Whizz in a blender until smooth.
Serve the pears with a jug of sauce or arrange on individual plates with a little of their syrup and a pool of Fresh Strawberry Coulis.

I hardly need say that a tofu cream adds extra luxury to this dessert. If you can get some fresh figs, they behave very well when given this treatment too!

Almond Cream

Makes about 750 ml
(1¼ pints/3 cups)

---

175 g (6 oz/2 cups) ground
* almonds*
300 ml (½ pint/1⅓ cups) soya
* milk*
1 teaspoon almond essence
50 g (2 oz/¼ cup) silken tofu
* (optional)*
2 tablespoons apple juice
* concentrate*

Blend until smooth.

Banana Cream

Makes about 750 ml
(1¼ pints/3 cups)

---

2 bananas
300 ml (½ pint/1 cup) soya
* milk*
3 tablespoons cooked brown rice
* or rice porridge*
1 level teaspoon grated nutmeg

Blend until smooth.

Italian Almond Pudding

Serves 4–6
Oven: 180°C/350°F/gas 4

---

450 g (1 lb/4 cups) chopped dessert apples
pinch of cinnamon
pinch of ground cloves
2 tablespoons apple juice or water

Cook the apples gently with the spices and apple juice or water until tender.

---

175 g (6 oz/1 cup) organic white flour
175 g (6 oz/1 cup) wholemeal (wholewheat) flour
100 g (4 oz/1 cup) chopped almonds

Sift the flours and mix well with the almonds in a large bowl.

---

100 g (4 oz/½cup) soya margarine
7 tablespoons clear honey
3 teaspoons almond essence

Melt gently together and add to the flour and almonds mixture in the bowl. Stir well. Turn into a deep ovenproof dish and spread the cooked apples over the top. Bake for approximately 1 hour.

Works well with other fruit – such as pears with nutmeg, fresh figs with cinnamon or cherries cooked with a vanilla pod (vanilla bean).

Maple Cream

*Makes about 1 litre
(1¾ pints/4 cups)*

225–275 g (8–10 oz/1½ cups)
  silken tofu
150 ml (¼ pint/⅔ cup) organic
  maple syrup
150 ml (¼ pint/⅔ cup) soya
  milk

Whizz in a blender until smooth.

Orange Spice Cream

*Makes about 1 litre
(1¾ pints/4 cups)*

225–275 g (8–10 oz/1½ cups)
  silken tofu
finely grated rind (zest) of 1 large
  orange
150 ml ¼ pint/⅔ cup) soya milk
1 heaped teaspoon ground mixed
  spice (apple pie spice)
1 level teaspoon ground cinnamon
2 tablespoons apple juice
  concentrate or clear honey or
  date syrup

Whizz in a blender until smooth.

Oat and Orangey Mince Pie

Serves 4–6
Oven: 180°C/350°F/gas 4

---

75 g (3 oz/⅓ cup) soya margarine
5 tablespoons olive oil
grated rind (zest) of 1 orange
450 g (1 lb/3 cups) wholemeal
  (wholewheat) flour, sifted
water, to mix

Mix the margarine, oil and orange rind (zest) into the flour, then stir in just enough water for the mixture to come together into a dough. Roll out and use to line 23-cm (8-in) flan tin.

---

450 g (1lb) organic sugar-free
  mincemeat or dates or dried
  fruit of your choice soaked in
  orange juice

Fill the pastry case with your chosen ingredients.

---

100 g (4 oz/1½ cups) oats
2 tablespoons clear honey
1 tablespoon sunflower or olive oil

Mix together and gently press onto the filling. Bake in the oven for 35–40 minutes.

Creamy Banana and Maple Gratinée

Serves 4–6
Oven: 220°C/425°F/gas 7

---

50 g (2 oz/⅓ cup) brown rice and 1 litre (1¾ pints/4 cups) soya milk

Simmer together for approximately 1 hour until the rice is soft.

---

300 ml (½ pint/1 cup) soya milk
3 teaspoons vanilla essence
75 g (3oz/½ cup) creamed coconut
4 tablespoons arrowroot, creamed to a runny paste with a little water

Bring gently to the boil, stirring with a whisk continually. Simmer for 5 minutes and stir into the rice pudding. You may find that you need to add a little more soya milk – it should be the consistency of thick custard.

---

6 ripe bananas, sliced
100 g (4 oz/½ cup) wheat flakes or oats
maple syrup, to serve

Spread the bananas out in a greased ovenproof dish. Pour over the creamy coconut topping, sprinkle with the wheat flakes or oats and drizzle with maple syrup. Bake in the oven for 10 minutes, until the top is golden.

Prune and Poppy Seed Tart

Serves 4–6
Oven: 180°C/350°F/gas 4

---

150 g (5 oz/1 cup) wholemeal
   (wholewheat) flour
150 g (5 oz/1 cup) organic white
   flour
50 g (2 oz/¼ cup) soya
margarine
85 ml (3 fl oz/scant ½ cup) olive
   oil
1 tablespoon clear honey
approximately 85 ml (3 fl oz/scant
   ½ cup) cold water

Sift the flours together into a large bowl. Mix in the margarine, oil and honey and enough water to form a workable pastry. Roll the pastry out and line a 25-cm (10-in) flan tin. Keep the trimmings and roll them out again. Cut into 2.5-cm (1-in) wide strips or decorative shapes.

---

225 g (8 oz/2 cups) poppy seeds
120 ml (¼ pint/½ cup) fresh
   orange juice
14 tablespoons set honey

Whizz to a smooth paste in a blender. You will need to keep stopping and scraping down the sides.

---

225 g (8 oz/1 generous cup) stoned
   (pitted) prunes
finely grated zest (peel) of 1
   orange
50 g (2 oz/½ cup) chopped walnuts
soya milk, for glazing

Soak the prunes in boiling water for 10 minutes, then drain and chop them.
Stir them into the poppy see mixture and spread over the base of the pastry case. Use the pastry strips or shapes to make a lattice or pattern on the top and glaze with a little soya milk.
Bake for approximately 1 hour and 10 minutes, until light golden brown.

Serve with vanilla cream.

Rice Pudding

Serves 4–6
Oven: 170°C/325°C/gas 3

---

75 g (3 oz/½ cup) organic brown rice
1 litre (1¾ pints/4 cups) soya milk

Put together in a heavy based pan and simmer very gently, covered, for 2 hours. There is no need to stir, but do make sure the heat is very low.
Alternatively, place the ingredients in a greased oven-proof casserole dish and bake, covered, for 2–3 hours. For the best result, though, make the Rice Pudding in a slow cooker, cooking for 4 hours or overnight.

This is very good with the addition of a vanilla pod (vanilla bean) or some grated nutmeg or dried fruit.

Stuffed Baked Apples with Blackberry Sauce

Serves 4
Oven: 180°C/350°F/gas 4

---

*4 medium sweet apples, cored
(Cox's or Russets are good)
100 g (4 oz/½ cup) finely ground
almonds
2 tablespoons set or clear
honey
pinch of cinnamon*

Stir and knead together to form a thick 'mouldable' mixture. Form into 4 little sausage shapes and push these down into the cored apples, leaving a little mound on the top of each. Place in a small, greased ovenproof dish that they just fit into, cover and bake for 1 hour and 30 minutes, or until soft but not breaking up.

---

*225 g (8 oz/1⅓ cups) fresh
blackberries
2 tablespoons honey or apple
juice concentrate
juice of 1 lemon*

While the apples are baking, bring the blackberries, honey or apple juice concentrate and lemon juice to a gentle boil in a heavy based pan. Cool and push through a strainer to remove the seeds.
Serve the apples hot or chilled on individual plates with a little pool of sauce beside them.

Vanilla Cream (see page 114) adds a wonderful finishing touch to this dessert.

Vanilla Cream

Makes about 1 litre (1¾ pints/4 cups)

225–275 g (8–10 oz/1½ cups)
  silken tofu
150 ml (¼ pint/⅔ cup) soya
  milk
3 teaspoons vanilla essence
2 teaspoons apple juice concentrate
  or 4 teaspoons clear honey

Whizz in a blender until smooth.

Coconut Cream

Makes about 400 ml (14 fl oz/1¾ cups)

---

25 g (1 oz/⅛ cup) creamed coconut
4 tablespoons hot water
300 ml (½ pint/1 cup) soya milk
1 tablespoon apple juice
  concentrate or honey (some
  honeys will make the cream
  thinner)

Dissolve the creamed coconut in the hot water.
Blend with the remaining ingredients until smooth.

Wholemeal Shortcrust Pastry (Wholewheat Pie Pastry)

Makes sufficient for two 25-cm (10-in) diameter pastry cases or one 30-cm (12-in) diameter double-crust pie

100 g (4 oz/½ cup) soya margarine
120 ml (4 fl oz/½ cup) olive or sunflower oil
450 g (1 lb/3 cups) wholemeal (wholewheat flour), sift out the bran
water, to mix

Mix the margarine and oil into the flour, and add just enough cold water to bind. Roll out on a floured surface, using the bran you have sifted out if you like.

To make a recognizable pastry does require the traditional 'half fat to flour' proportions, so this cannot really be described as a low-fat food. I include this recipe as it is, rather than lower the fat proportions as, personally, I would rather have really nice pastry occasionally than one that is less delicious more often! At the Centre we make a pastry dish just once a week and keep the rest of the meal fat free.

This recipe is a good all rounder and is varied easily by using half and half brown and organic white flour or fine oatmeal or soya flour or, if you are feeling brave, rice flour (the resulting pastry is difficult to roll, but tastes good).

For sweet dishes, add the zest of an orange and a teaspoon of honey for a delicious sweet pastry. Careful, though, as honey in the oven browns quickly. For savoury dishes, add herbs or ground sesame seeds, a dash of sesame oil or a teaspoon of tamari, as the mood takes you.

Cakes and Cookies

Banana and Hazelnut Cake

Makes one 500-g (1-lb) loaf
Oven: 180°C/350°F/gas 4

---

450 g (1 lb/3 cups) ripe bananas,
*   mashed*
50 g (2 oz/½ cup) hazelnuts,
*   chopped*
150 ml (¼ pint/½ cup) sunflower
*   or olive oil*
100 g (4 oz/⅔ cup) raisins
75 g (3 oz/1 cup) rice flour
1 teaspoon almond essence
*   (optional) or vanilla essence*

Mix together well and turn into a greased 500 g (1 lb) loaf tin. Bake for 50–60 minutes. Let cool in the tin before serving. As with many eggless, sugar-free, low-fat cakes, it definitely benefits from being wrapped in foil or being kept in an airtight container overnight.

Experiment with substituting almonds or walnuts, Brazil nuts or hazelnuts, and dates or apricots or chopped figs for the raisins.

Carrot Cake

*Makes one 20-cm (8-in)
diameter round cake
Oven: 180°C/350°F/gas 4*

---

*100 g (4 oz/1 cup) soya margarine
150 ml (¼ pint/½ cup) sunflower
   oil
8 tablespoons honey
450 g (1 lb/3 cups) finely grated
   carrots
1 teaspoon vanilla essence
finely grated zest (rind) of 1 orange*

Melt together gently over a low heat, then remove
the pan from the heat.

---

*450 g (1 lb/4 cups) wholemeal
   (wholewheat) flour
2 tablespoons ground cinnamon
1 tablespoon mixed spice
   (apple pie spice)
½ teaspoon ground nutmeg
2 tablespoons potassium-based
   baking powder*

Sift all these ingredients together and mix into
the carrot mixture.
Turn into a greased 20-cm (8-in) diameter round cake
tin and bake for approximately 1 hour and 15
minutes. It is done when a skewer inserted into the
centre comes out more or less clean and the cake has
shrunk from the sides. Let cool in tin before turning
out. This cake is best kept wrapped in foil or in an
airtight container for a day before slicing.

Date and Banana Cookies

Makes 18–20
Oven: 200°C/375°F/gas 6

75 g (3 oz/½ cup) dried dates,
   finely chopped
75 g (3 oz/⅔ cup) walnuts, finely
   chopped
3 medium bananas, mashed
175 g (6 oz/2 cups) oats
150 ml (¼ pint/½ cup) olive or
   sunflower oil
1 teaspoon vanilla essence

Mix everything together really well and put tablespoons of the mixture onto an oiled baking sheet. Flatten them down a bit and bake for about 20 minutes, until golden.

Currant and Raisin Squares

Makes about 12
Oven: 180°C/350°F/gas 4

---

150 g (5 oz/1 cup) raisins
50 g (2 oz/⅓ cup) currants

Whizz in a blender until finely chopped.

---

150 g (5 oz/1 cup) wholemeal
  (wholewheat) flour
75 g (3 oz/1 cup) oats
4 tablespoons sunflower or olive oil
pinch of ground cinnamon
120–175 ml (4–6 fl oz/½–⅔ cup)
  water

Add to the blender, using just enough water to make it all hold together.
Press the mixture down well into a greased baking sheet approximately 20 cm (8 in) square and bake for approximately 30 minutes. Cut into squares while still warm, but leave in the tin to cool before serving.

Quick Oat and Raisin Cookies

Makes 16–18
Oven: 200°C/375°F/gas 6

---

250 g (9 oz/3 cups) oats
225 g (8 oz/1½ cups) rice flour
150 g (6 oz/1 cup) raisins
75 g (3 oz/1 cup) chopped nuts of
  your choice
4 tablespoons olive or sunflower oil
1 tablespoon clear honey or apple
  juice concentrate
apple juice, to mix

Mix together well, using just enough apple juice to make a mixture with a soft 'dropping' consistency. Bake tablespoons of the mixture flattened into rough cookie shapes on oiled baking sheets for about 20 minutes.

Chewy Apricot and Honey Bars

Makes 20–24
Oven: 180°C/350°F/gas 4

---

*finely grated zest (peel) and juice of
    2 oranges*
*225 g (8 oz/1 cup) chopped dried
    apricots*

Bring to a gentle boil, remove the pan from the heat,
cover and let stand for 15 minutes.

---

6 tablespoons honey
150 ml (¼ pint/½ cup) oil
150 g (5 oz/1½ cups) oats
*150 g (5 oz/1 cup) wholemeal
    (wholewheat) flour*
50 g (2 oz/½ cup) sesame seeds
*2 pinches mixed spice
    (apple pie spice)*
150 g (5 oz/1 cup) raisins
*150 g (5 oz/1 cup) almonds,
    toasted for 5 minutes in a hot
    oven and ground or chopped*

Stir into the apricot mixture in the order the
ingredients are listed here, beginning with the
honey and ending with the almonds. Press the
mixture down into a greased baking sheet
approximately 25 by 33 cm (9 by 13 in) and bake
for 25–30 minutes.
Let the mixture cool completely before cutting
into fingers.

Frosted Carob Cake

*Makes one 23-cm (9-in)
    diameter round cake
    or a 450-g (1-lb) loaf
Oven: 180°C/350°F/gas 4*

*75 g (3 oz/½ cup) carob
    powder*
50 g (2 oz/⅓ cup) soya flour
*50 g (2 oz/⅓ cup) wholemeal
    (wholewheat) flour or organic
    white flour*
*1 tablespoon potassium-based
    baking powder*

Sift everything together, holding the sieve (sifter) high over the bowl to incorporate as much air as possible.

*100 g (4 oz/⅔ cup) raisins or
    chopped dates*
*50 g (2 oz/⅔ cup) dessicated
    (shredded) coconut*
*150 ml (¼ pint/½ cup) apple
    juice*
*1 tablespoon natural date syrup
    or apple juice concentrate*

Add these to the dry ingredients. Stir quickly and turn into a 23-cm (8-in) diameter round oiled cake tin or a 450-g (1-lb) loaf tin. Bake for about 1 hour. Let cool before spreading the topping over.

50 g (2 oz/⅓ cup) carob powder
3 tablespoons light tahini
*2 tablespoons apple juice
    concentrate*
apple juice, to mix

Blend to a thick, smooth cream, then spread over the top of the cake.

Fruit and Nut Slice

Makes about 12
Oven: 190°C/375°F/gas 5

---

150 g (5 oz/1 cup) raisins 150 g (5 oz/1 cup) mixed nuts of your choice	Whizz together for a couple of seconds in a blender.

---

4 teaspoons pear and apple spread
    (or other fruit concentrate)
85 ml (3 fl oz/scant ½ cup)
    sunflower oil
	Add to the blender and whizz briefly again.

---

75 g (3 oz/1 cup) oats 150 g (5 oz/1cup) organic white flour	Add to the blender and give another quick whizz.

---

85 ml (3 fl oz/scant ½ cup) cold water	Add to the blender and whizz to make quite a sticky mixture. Press it into a greased quiche tin or baking sheet, approximately 20 cm (8 in) square. Bake for about 30 minutes, or until nicely browned. Slice and let cool before serving.

 These slices store very well in an airtight container and can easily be varied by exchanging the raisins for other dried fruits (such as apricots), and by popping in a few seeds, such as sesame or sunflower.

Healthy Store Cupboard

A quick checklist to help you with your new style of shopping:

Nuts and Seeds

alfalfa seeds (for sprouting)
almonds
Brazil nuts
cashew nuts
hazelnuts
macadamia nuts
pecan nuts
pine kernels
poppy seeds
pumpkin seeds
sesame seeds
sunflower seeds
walnuts

Dried Fruits

apricots
currants
dates
figs
prunes
raisins
sultanas

Dried Herbs

basil
bay leaves
chives, parsley and coriander are better fresh
mint
oregano
sage
tarragon
thyme

Spices

cardamom pods
cayenne pepper

cinnamon sticks
cloves
garam masala
ground cinnamon
ground coriander
ground cumin
nutmeg
star anise
turmeric powder
whole coriander seed
whole cumin seed
whole yellow/black mustard seed

Other Flavourings

almond essence
cider vinegar
low salt bouillon powder
low salt yeast spread
malt extract
miso paste
shoyu soy sauce
silken tofu
soya milk
tahini (sesame paste)
tamari soy sauce
tomato purée
vanilla essence

Fats and Oils

cold pressed nut oils
cold pressed olive oil
cold pressed sunflower oil
vegan soya margarine

Grains

bulgar
couscous
oats
quince
wheat berries (grain)
whole brown rice

Beans, Pulses and Pasta

aduki beans
blackeye beans
brown lentils
butter beans

cannelli beans
chick peas
flageolet beans
green lentils
mung beans
red lentils
rice, millet or buckwheat pasta
wholewheat pasta shapes
yellow split peas

Sweet Flavourings

apple juice concentrate
carob powder
date syrup
honey
maple syrup
organic apple juice
organic fruit concentrates
organic sugar-free jams and spreads
soya milk
sugar-free mincemeat

Flours

100 per cent wholewheat flour
arrowroot
brown rice flour
maize meal
organic white flour
polenta
soya flour
spelt wheat flour

Index

Healing Foods

How to nurture yourself and fight illness

Dr Rosy Daniel

Why should you change your diet? The chances are you are overfed
and undernourished – finding comfort in rich, sweet and processed foods
which will make you vulnerable to many serious illnesses. Now is the time
to make some healthy new choices when you buy and cook food.

Healing Foods will inspire and instruct anybody interested in preserving
their health and give hope and direction to people who want to help their bodies
fight disease. Dr Rosy Daniel offers information and solutions to
help you make the change, gradually, to balanced and nutritious eating.
The book includes menus, ideas and advice both for those who have been
weakened by illness or its treatment and for those who wish to prevent
illness in the first place. Every page will give you the information and
inspiration to think about the food you eat in a new way.

'Simple to understand, clear and accurate. Rosy Daniel's *Healing Foods*
cuts through all the confusion about how to eat well for life. I highly
recommend it.' – *Leslie Kenton*